SWIFT IN THE NIGHT

and other
Tales of Field and Wood

Swift in the Night

AND OTHER
TALES OF FIELD AND WOOD

BY WILLIAM BYRON MOWERY

Coward-McCann, Inc.   New York

Foreword

THIS is a book of the Outdoors and its creatures. Of the fox, its bairns, its hunting ways. Of the shy, friendly wolf and the truth about this much-maligned animal. Of the rabbit, the woodchuck, the waxwing and the great northern grizzly.

With a few exceptions the adventures recounted in this book—the amazing things observed, the delightful things done—are such as lie open to nearly everybody. Emphatically this strange, extra-human world, as strange as any trip to another planet, is not limited to the trained biologist or professional scientist. I myself am at most only a home-made naturalist, and the time I can spend outdoors is only such as is left over from the business of making a living. On winter afternoons, when the day's work is done, I get back into the white, silent hills for an hour or two, afoot or a-ski, and see how my friends are faring in this stern and rigorous year-time. And on summer evenings, when the sun lies slant and golden over the woods and lush fields, I have an intolerable itch to be out the back door and gone.

To "know a bank where the wild thyme blows" will pay no taxes, to be sure. The lure, the magic and the value of the world outdoors lie deeper than that, deeper than I have words to express. It is a world where we find a firm and reassuring constancy, in contrast to the unsettled roil and bewildering flux of human affairs. A world that gives us a healthy and needed respite from the unavoidable strains and pressures of modern life. A world where for a brief while we can forget personal troubles and international crises alike.

There is never, says Thoreau, any bad news at Walden. During the past half century America has changed from a pioneering land and rural-minded people into a highly industrialized nation and a population largely city-born and city-oriented. However richly she may have gained in many respects, she has suffered one great loss, subtle but profound. Those generations of Americans who went before us had a knowledge of Nature, a love for it, a nearness to it, a communion with it, which we today almost totally lack. In the writings of New England's Longfellow, Emerson, Bryant, of Whitman, of the Midwest's Hamlin Garland and the early Willa Cather, Nature played an important role. But in present-day American writing, engrossed with Freudian themes and so-called "realism" and so fond of depicting human life as a rat race, Nature is almost wholly neglected and ignored.

Of individuals and of nations which have become overly intellectual, overly citified and industrialized, it has been said, "They have been drawn above the earth and hang there withering," and to a certain extent this is indeed true. Those who live entirely in the concrete canyons and other man-made artificialities of the metropolis have been cut off from a precious heritage. But even in the most confirmed city dweller I have often sensed, as others have mentioned, a deep and inarticulate thirst for the world that the Lord made and for a life that is nearer the earth. I hope that the pieces in this book will help some people to assuage that thirst a little, vicariously; but much more do I hope that my own experiences and delights will lead a few readers, here and there, to go out and do likewise and to have those exquisite pleasures at first hand.

On my desk lies a snapshot of a husky young biologist who is a Point-Four adviser in Pakistan. Sitting in front of his headquarters building, he is feeding a fledgling bird and has half a dozen other birds perched on his arms and shoulders. The grin on his face indicates he is pleased as punch with himself. At the bottom of the picture he wrote just one word to me—"Remember?"

Indeed I do remember, and what a story that snapshot tells! Many years ago, during the period I describe in "The Lord's Tiny Poultry," our neighborhood was plagued by a certain little boy of eight, a little toughie if ever there was one. His pastime of hunting up bird nests and wringing the necks of the fledglings was only one of his unprepossessing activities, and it was generally prophesied thereabouts that he was a born bad 'un who would come to no good end. In reality he was merely a neglected and spiritually homeless little boy, with the bellyful of fire that all little boys have or ought to have.

One time, as a calculated move to protect our flock of tame birds, I gave him an English-sparrow fledgling to take home and promised him a dime a day if he would feed and take care of it for me. Ten days passed. Then the small scalawag came around one morning and asked if he could maybe buy the sparrow, and he offered me his little fistful of hard-won dimes if I'd let him have the sparrow as his own. It goes without saying that never again did he twist a fledgling's neck off. In fact, he became a trusted helper with our flock of tame birds, and from that he began going along with us on our country trips. Before moving away, I passed him along to a university associate, a zoologist, who fostered and guided his growing interest in the field sciences.

As you probably have guessed, that little toughie grew up to be the biologist of the Pakistan snapshot.

The moral of this experience—and I could cite a dozen similar instances—is simply this: a parent can give a child no greater gift than to awaken and encourage in him an interest toward the outdoors and Nature, with its many aspects—plants, flowers, birds, insects, animals. The enduring influence of this interest I have seen again and again, and always it has been wholly good. In childhood it is a fascinating sort of play, which will keep little people absorbed for hours at a time. In stormy and bewildered adolescence it is a uniquely steadying hobby and interest; a greatly needed leaven against undue preoccupation with the other sex and similar inclinations of the hot-rod set. And in adult life it continues to be an unfailing pleasure and zest, abiding with us when troubled times come on and other pleasures are scarce.

It seems to me that today, when the comics, many books, and even the ether waves are so full of violence and brassy clangor, the gentling influence of Nature pursuits is especially needed by young people and especially valuable for them.

So, get your child a few of the fine, inexpensive Nature books we have today. Get him a few simple items of equipment, like a butterfly net, an observation cage, a cheap microscope and the Nature-study ensembles which the biology houses sell; and encourage him in every way you can to know and like the outdoors.

And remember that we do not need a Rocky Mountain or a "forest primeval" for genuine Nature study and delights. Almost any little patch of earth and tangle of greenery will do. Once Agassiz remarked to a friend that he had spent the summer traveling, and when his friend asked where he'd gone, Agassiz replied, "I got halfway across my back yard."

In this book you will notice that I often speak of animals as having, at least in a rudimentary way, certain emotions and traits which are sometimes regarded as exclusively human, such as loneliness, pride, parental love, jealousy, a sense of dignity, a sense of proprietorship, and so on.

I can hear some people saying: "Aha! Anthropomorphizing, that fellow!" That's the bad word these days—anthropomorphizing. Ascribing human attributes to animals. Ever since the Huxley era this interpretation of animal life and behavior has been branded as rank heresy, and the writer or the naturalist guilty of it has found himself cast into outer darkness.

Well now, how about this?

As a part of the brash and iconoclastic materialism characterizing so much modern thinking, it has been the fashion since Huxley's time to describe animals as nothing but automata and to consider animal behavior as nothing but chemical reactions, tropisms and rigid instincts. Similarly it has been the fashion to describe human life and behavior as nothing but a complex of ego, id and physical processes. Indeed, the adherents of this school of thought have recently been dubbed the "Nothing-Butters."

To paraphrase one of our present-day philosophers, man has been pushed down to the animal level and so animals have had to be pushed still farther down the mechanistic scale.

If you are one of those who felt that this materialistic interpretation of animal life was wrong; if it violated what you saw outdoors with your own eyes; if you believed that Nature is far, far from being a cruel struggle-for-survival arena, where everything is adjusted by brute force —well, you can take heart now and be of good cheer. Help is coming. And coming from science itself. From scientists working in animal psychology. Working under strict laboratory regimen and arriving at conclusions which leave no room for doubt or argument. And they tell us, these authorities in their field, that all the traits and emotions I mentioned above, plus others still more recondite, do exist in animals, and that there is scarcely one basic human characteristic which cannot be observed, at least in proto-form, among the higher animals.

In a brilliantly reasoned and documented essay, Professor Katt summarizes the work of himself and other European psychologists, and of such commanding figures as Professor Yerkes in America. There are, says Professor Katt, three levels of behavior—instinctive, emotional, rational. In a technical sense animals do not operate on the rational level; that is, they do not possess reasoning powers. But on the instinctive and emotional levels they are very well equipped indeed; in fact some of them, in some respects, are better equipped than man. And on these two levels, instinct and emotion, there is room for intelligent action and for behavior based on deep, complex emotions.

I, for one, am profoundly glad that the dreary and bullying philosophy of the "Nothing-Butters" is at last on its way out. It will be some time, I'm sure, before they realize that their boasted "realism" was nothing except a frame of mind, a superficial and obnoxious frame of mind, and some time before their influence is fully spent. But their day of power is over.

Lastly, a word of explanation and my acknowledgments.

"Swift in the Night" is the one purely fictional selection in this book. I chose to cast this material in the short-story mold because, as every writer knows, fiction can sometimes convey a deeper truth, a deeper understanding and insight, than a factual telling. This story, I hope, will cause you to put aside your humanhood for a little time and see, as more than one of my magazine readers expressed it, "what it feels like to be a fox."

"Sangamon Sketches" includes four selections from a decade of outdoor work and publications while I lived in Illinois. "Northland Trails," devoted entirely to the wolf, comprises experiences and field studies of mine in the Canadian sub-Arctic, where I spent parts of a dozen summers gathering material for my fiction of the Northwest Territories and also doing some collecting for museums and scientific institutes. "Catskill Adventures" covers my latest period, during which I have been teaching at New York University and authoring stories, articles and books.

All the pieces in this volume appeared originally in magazines and I wish to thank those editors and publishers for their permission to use these selections here. Specifically, thanks are due to *Audubon* for "The Mystery of the Big

Hop"; to *Sports Afield* for "Mushroom Hunting," " 'Seng Hunter" and "Wild Salads"; to *Saga* for "The Battle of Red Rock Bluff" and "Circus on the Hillside"; to *Bluebook* for "Saga of the Wolf"; to *Country Gentleman* for "The New Look in Animal Homes"; to *Reader's Digest* for "The Lord's Tiny Poultry"; to *Elks Magazine* for "Loafer Wolf" and "The Whistle Pig Plays It Safe"; and to *The Saturday Evening Post* for "Swift in the Night" and "Smoky and the Golden Vixen."

William Byron Mowery

Warwick, New York

Contents

SWIFT IN THE NIGHT

Swift in the Night

IN the clump of small sassafras trees halfway up Laurel Slope, the red-fox vixen was crouching at the mouth of her den and restlessly awaiting daybreak. Below her, Laurel Valley was still a trough of darkness, and from the rocky hills to the west the ghostly hooting of the horned owls was still drifting down. But the chill, sparkling April night was almost over. The eastern stars were dimming out, and in the old sedge fields of Laurel Slope the first birdcalls were breaking the clean dark silence.

For the red vixen the night had been long and painshot. She had not gone hunting since her cubs were killed, and hunger was needling her sharply. Her swollen dugs, unrelieved for two nights and a day, were throbbing and fevered. And the abrupt shattering of her usual rounds—hunting by night, suckling the cubs, leading them on their first few steps from the den, and watching over the place by day from the old maple snag—had left her muddled and bewildered.

The vixen's den in the sassafras clump was merely an enlarged woodchuck hole, with an apron of bare dirt at the mouth to give the cubs a dust wallow and a patch of sun. On five successive springs the vixen had come there at her heavy period and whelped, and four times she had reared her young successfully. The den was far enough from the bottom farms to be fairly safe from dogs and berry-pickers, yet near enough that the vixen, a swift and silent creature of the night, could reach down to the good hunting of the cornfields and meadows.

But on this fifth spring a sudden, wanton death had visited the clump of sassafras. A large tom wildcat, savage from an unhealed buckshot wound, had appeared on Laurel Slope without warning, had happened upon the den at twilight and caught the four cubs playing in a patch of sumac just below the hole. When the vixen returned from hunting, her cubs were scattered dead in the sumac and the hillside reeked with the big-cat smell.

Two of the cubs had been so mangled that they seemed unnatural things and she had not touched them. But the other two she had carried up to the den and laid on the apron of dirt, and she was crouching beside them now. Their small bodies were long since rigid, their black forelegs stuck out stiffly, their puppy fur was coated with hoarfrost.

The sense of guarding her young while the big-cat smell still lingered had bound the vixen there throughout two nights and a day. Occasionally she would still nudge the two cubs and lick the hoarfrost from their fur. But she was beginning to feel an alienation toward them, the aliena-

tion that lies between the quick and the dead, and hunger
was prodding her to make a foraging trip down to a valley
farmstead.

In the frosty silence a sudden, muffled noise a hundred
yards out the hillside brought the vixen flashing to her feet,
sharp ears up, her nose questioning the air. Then she dis-
tinguished the click of hoofs, the swish of brush, and knew
it was only the troupe of five deer that bedded by day in
the aspen thicket higher up the slope. But this return from
their night rounds meant it was time for her to reconnoiter
and then start on her dangerous foray down to the valley.

She turned and glided shadowlike out to the old leaning snag three rods from the den. One effortless leap and
she stood poised on the broken top of it a dozen feet above
the ground, her keen nose reading the night around her.
There was no fresh taint of the wildcat on the air, or of
dog or man, and no unusual noises in the dark buckbrush
of the hillside.

Satisfied that her den was safe, she turned her attention
down across the treetops to the bottoms—to a farmstead
lying between the valley road and the foot of Laurel Slope.
The ground wind of dawn, flowing down from the pine
uplands like a thin, invisible stream, was wrong for her reconnoitering; her nose could tell her nothing and her ears
not much. But everything about the farm seemed as usual
for that hour. The converted barn that housed the flock of
laying hens was lighted up, but the dwelling and other
buildings were dark. The loudmouthed brindle dog in the

picket pen barked at a passing truck; the windmill creaked slowly; the heavy old horse stomped and coughed under the apple tree.

Much as the red vixen dreaded to go near the dangerous man-place, there were crises in the whelping period when hunger took her down to the farmstead willy-nilly. Snow-spitting April and early May, before the rabbit numbers were renewed by the spring and the birds returned in the migrant spate, were immemorially the lean moon of the fox tribe, yet this was her time of greatest need, the suckling time, when the cubs kept her drained and gaunt. With no food hoard or other resources, she had only her teeth and wits by which to glean a living for herself and her young, night by night, through the frosty fields and barren woods. When this regular hunting failed, then the cackling of the fat clumsy fowls set her prancing and slavering.

By night the fowls at the farmstead were locked up tight, and by day the man, the shotgun and the dog with the blaring mouth made the place forbidden to a fox with any caution. But by long scouting and watching, the vixen had hit on a shrewdly-timed maneuver that yielded her a chicken whenever she was hunger-driven.

The gray in the eastern sky warned her to hurry. She sprang lightly down from the snag and swung out to the den, where she paused to nuzzle the cubs again. Out of habit she stepped a few feet away from the hole, looked back and gave the two cubs a snarl, which meant that she was leaving on a hunt and they were not to follow. Then she was gone.

Wraithlike through the deerbush and the belts of scrub timber, she dropped down the long slope in a succession of swift runs and reconnoitering halts, choosing her zigzag path in accordance with the ancient wisdoms of the fox tribe.

Near the foot of Laurel Slope she came to a little half-acre clearing where a deep spring welled up through the shield rock. From several directions worn animal trails converged on the spillway pool of slightly salt water. A trim spike buck stood there drinking.

As the vixen skirted the little clearing she caught the scent of a dog-fox near at hand and stopped short. Then she recognized it as the scent of old Carry One, her erstwhile mate, and from the brush on the other side he came ambling across toward her.

He was a large, oldish red, with shrewd, quizzical eyes and an air of self-confidence. As he trotted across he carried his left rear leg in a jaunty fashion. Years ago, as a brash yearling, he had caught the foot in a trap, and had got into the carrying habit while the slow bone wounds were healing. But it was only a habit; when he needed to run, the leg went down and he flashed an amazing speed, his flight as airy as a swallow's coursing. Of ripe experience and skinful of tricks, he was probably the wisest creature and most sagacious hunter on Laurel Slope.

The vixen and old Carry One had been mates throughout their maturity, in the loose fox way, and he had sired all five of her litters. During the breeding week they would range together through the snowy winter hills to the west, and after that he would follow her out to the den on Laurel Slope. When the cubs came, he was strictly *non grata* around the sassafras clump. If he ventured near, the vixen would drive him back with a snarling rush and a slash of her punishing teeth. But he would hang around, nevertheless, and he had his uses. He would bring kills and lay them in the brush out beyond the old snag, and when dogs roved too near the den, he would cleverly cross their noses and draw them off in another direction.

While the spike buck unconcernedly flicked its ears at the two foxes, old Carry One approached the vixen with the boldness of long acquaintance. But the vixen stopped him short with a growl and a show of fangs. In the past several months he had become somewhat of a stranger, for they had not consorted since the wintertime, back in the hills. They had mated then, but after staying with her only a few hours, old Carry One had disappeared. Later she had struck his trail in the snow, alongside the trail of a young, smallish vixen. For a whole week afterward she kept meeting those two trails, always together, through miles of the wintry woods. Still later, old Carry One and the young, odd-colored vixen had shown up on Laurel Slope and the vixen had denned in a rocky hollow a mile from the sassafras clump.

Sniffing curiously, old Carry One walked around the vixen twice, then sat down and looked at her shrewdly, as though he understood her swollen dugs, her gauntness and the faint linger of wildcat smell.

With more important business urging her, the vixen broke off the meeting and trotted away down a deer path. Old Carry One got up, circled around her and crossed her nose, as she had seen him do to draw dogs from a course. It was as though he knew she was making another poultry foray and was uneasy. Not that he himself did not visit the bottoms. He liked to scout around the dark, sleeping farms, catching mice at the grain sheds and picking off rabbits in the apple orchards. In the lush fall, when hunting was easy and his blood ran strong, he liked to stir up the excitable farm dogs, get them to chase him into the briar hills, and there bedevil them to a frenzy with his baffle tricks. But never would he molest the poultry flocks. That wisdom the trap had taught him.

Twice he circled ahead of the red vixen and crossed her nose. When she paid no attention to him, he finally sat down on the path; and she left him there, watching her with his shrewd, quizzical eyes.

Beyond the last woods at the foot of Laurel Slope, she darted down along a pasture fence to a willow brook. As she was slipping up along the small stream toward the farmstead, she unexpectedly came upon the scent of old Carry One's mate, the honey-colored vixen. The scent made her hackle up; she considered the farm her own hunting ground. But she was more curious than angry, and she followed the trail a little distance each way, studying the signs with her nose.

The tracks were of yesterday and rather faint. The long leaps were those of a fox in hasty, straightaway flight. The feathers and driblets of blood meant a freshly killed chicken, partly eaten. In a general way the red vixen knew that yesterday in broad daylight, after the sun had swept up the hoarfrost and dew, the other vixen had caught a chicken at the farmyard and had started to eat it in the little marsh. But she had been flushed by the man or dog, and had fled, taking the rest of her kill with her.

Vaguely disquieted, the vixen leaped the brook by the small footlog and circled up against the low orchard hillside for a thorough reconnoitering.

In the graying light she halted in a clump of chokecherry and looked down at the dark buildings two hundred yards away. She could not locate the brindle dog; he was not barking around in his pen, as he had been an hour before, and this made her uneasy. But everything else was the same as on her previous trips. There was no light in the farmhouse, no sign that the man was stirring yet. The flock of layers were cackling away in the barn. The dozen stray fowls that roosted in the old apple tree near the pullet sheds were flapping their wings and getting ready to fly down. Over the little marsh that reached to within fifty feet of the sheds hung a low gray blanket of ground fog.

At a crouching run the vixen whisked down into the

reeds and fog, and headed for the upper end of the marsh. She moved swiftly till the reeds began thinning out. Then she slowed down, crouching lower and lower, till finally she bellied up behind the last tussock and lay quiet there, tensed for her strike and getaway.

The dozen or so chickens in the apple tree, the only fowls not behind lock and bar, were the ones she had been preying on. At evening all the others trooped into their proper sheds and sat in meek rows on the roosting poles, but that dozen still had a wisp of their native jungle spirit and preferred the tree roost, under the moon and stars. They always flew high up, beyond reach of the man's prod pole, and at dawn they came down early, before the man and dog were out. As the vixen had learned by her careful scouting, that little time at daybreak was the one chink in the twenty-four hours at the farmstead.

She was worried by the unusual silence of the dog. Also, her alert eyes noticed that a window of the feed shed stood open, which always before had been shut. But after studying it and seeing nothing suspicious, she turned her attention to the fidgety chickens, which would be flying down from the tree at any moment.

In the gray, broadening light, the stars had faded, and the high streaks of mare's-tail were turning rose from the first sun shafts. In the old beeches behind the orchard the squirrels had come out of their den holes and were scrabbling up and down the tree trunks.

An old rooster flapped out of the apple tree, crowed,

and began foraging. One by one the others followed, till they were all down. As they scattered here and there, the nearest to the marsh was a young rooster, and the vixen fixed her burning eyes on him. When he was twenty feet from the tussock, she sprang.

She covered the distance like a blur of red, seized the chicken, killed it neatly with a brain-bite and picked it up, to whirl and vanish into the marsh as before. But this morning the danger stirred up by the other vixen's foray lashed out at her—through that open window. At the moment she was turning she saw an explosive flare in the darkness of the shed. A hot, stabbing jolt struck her in the rump, another seared across the top of her neck, and the heavy *kroom* of a shotgun battered against her ears.

For a moment the vixen was terrified by the sudden blare and the hot jolt. The man in the shed yelled. The brindle dog, which had been so silent, came scrambling through the window and tearing across toward her. Recovering herself, the vixen dropped the chicken, whirled and darted for the marsh. The gun *kroomed* again and a spatter as of gale-driven sleet tore up the sod to one side of her. But no more of the stabbing things hit, and then she was back in the marsh, vanishing into the reeds and gray mist.

At full flight she raced the length of the swamp, skimmed up a grassy bank through the old beeches, crossed a briary pasture and corn-stubble field, and flew on and on, not slowing or looking back till she hit the brook again a mile below the farmstead. There she halted behind a screen of willows to watch and listen for pursuers. The pain in her rump had dulled; she gave it a quick lick or two and paid it no more attention.

As she stood watching, she was not a motionless, rigid object, of telltale animal outline. Instead she kept swaying her head and shoulders very slowly, slightly, in a motion that blended her with the willows—a peculiar, flowing movement like a slow wind wave in the grass.

She saw nothing of her enemies. Up near the farmstead the brindle dog was yelping around through the beeches, running her trail forward a piece and then backward a piece. At the different farms half a dozen dogs had been roused and were barking but none of them came to lend a nose to the brindle.

When the vixen was sure she was not being closely pursued, she started on, down along the brook. Her straightaway burst to get out of immediate danger was over. Now she had to keep enemies from following her back to the den of helpless cubs, and she began throwing baffles into her trail. For half a mile she kept leaping back and forth across the brook at its wide places. Then she cut over to the foot of Laurel Slope, headed directly away from her den and began doubling back, dodging in and out of holes, and following up shallow brooks.

It was nearly mid-morning when she got back to the deep-rock spring. As she halted there for a last reconnoitering, she caught the fresh scent of old Carry One again, close at hand. Her nose indicated that he was in a patch of thin brush just across the open space, but she was several moments making him out. He was not standing motionless, but swaying slightly, with that slow, eye-baffling movement that was like a wind wave in the grass.

Instead of coming over to her, old Carry One trotted down to her fresh trail and began crossing and recrossing it in a businesslike way, to muddle it up for any pursuers. It was as though he had known about the open window and silent dog, and had heard the *kroom*, and had waited there to see if she would come back. . . .

The habit of guarding her young by day kept the vixen close to her den as the forenoon passed and the afternoon dragged slowly along. Except for a few hasty looks at the dead cubs, she spent the hours stretched out on the snag top, patiently enduring her hunger and swollen dugs.

But the ties that held her to the den were fraying out and near the snapping point. The two small forms at the den mouth, unmoving and unanswering, were rapidly becoming alien things, and her awareness of them was dimming.

Her fright that morning, on top of the disaster to her cubs, had sharpened her dislike for Laurel Slope and the valley. Always she had come there unwillingly, to have adequate game when she was suckling cubs and teaching them to hunt for themselves. To her the valley meant fearful, unpredictable things like the *krooming* gun, toothed jump traps, strand wire that stunned like a splinter of lightning, the bitter white powder concealed in a tidbit that once had doubled her into knots, and now the overhanging threat of the big cat prowling somewhere on the slope. But there were none of these things in the timbered hills to the west, her winter range. There the old forest was undisturbed and the day itself was dim in the rocky hollows and heavy pine woods. All this was pulling at her to leave the den and Laurel Slope as soon as night came, and go back to the wild highlands.

In the early afternoon old Carry One came wandering up from the direction of the hollow and loitered for a while in the sedge fields and clumps of second growth. He seemed to be at loose ends, for some reason; not hunting or turning an enemy away from the other vixen's den, but merely drifting around restlessly. He would not venture close even with the cubs dead, but kept strictly to the distance he had learned was safe. After a while he wandered back toward the hollow.

Down at the farmstead the man burned off the little marsh in the dry mid-afternoon, so that no more foxes would slip up to the poultry yard unseen. Then he resumed his plowing above the orchard, with the brindle dog following in the furrows and chasing killdeers across the freshly turned soil.

When the ground wind started flowing up from the sun-warmed valley, it brought the red vixen the faint yapping of a fox cub in the rocky hollow. Somewhat like the wail of a cub that had followed its dam away from the den and was lost, the yapping stirred her curiosity. But it was a cold, hostile curiosity. She had had a number of hot fights with the other vixen over hunting grounds that spring, and usually had taken a painful slashing from the fierce younger fox, and out of this archaic struggle for food had grown a bitter feud. For the honey-colored vixen, her den, her whelps and even the scent of her on old Carry One, the red vixen had a bristling enmity.

Off and on with the varying breezes she kept hearing the yapping the rest of the afternoon, but she gave it little attention. The confusion that had followed the shattering of her rounds was giving way to one clear purpose—to get back to the wild, secluded uplands. The pull of the pine ranges, with their twilight hollows and booming of grouse and untainted winds, was as insistent as the constant small ache in her rump. The hunting was lean in the uplands, but the valley had too many hateful dangers. From her own experiences with those dangers and from the monotonous disasters that had happened each year to her cubs when they were nearly grown, the vixen had an obscure sense of some evil about the valley. She felt it only in a dim way, as something unnatural and mysterious, but it was real enough. In the easy hunting of the late summer and fall, her young and other young and even some of the older foxes lost their keen, wild hardness, and when the lean times came they fell to foraging around the farmsteads, and so perished.

By sundown the vixen was hearing the yapping of the

three other cubs in the rocky hollow. Several times she stood up, pointing her sharp ears in that direction, and probed the air with her nose for some answer to her curiosity, but she smelled nothing and the puzzle remained.

A vagrant wind finally brought her the outside edge of a scent. It was of her enemy, the honey-colored vixen. Not the ordinary odor of her enemy fighting or hunting, or the mating scent, but the pungent muskiness that foxes give off only in rare extremity, as in life-or-death battle. The tantalizing whiff puzzled the red vixen even more than the plaintive calling of the cubs.

In the first hush of owl dusk she sprang down from the snag and shook off the stiffness of her long vigil. She glanced once toward the den in the sassafras, where she had whelped for five springs, but her interest in it and in the two fuzzy things that lay there was so nearly extinguished that she did not go out for a last look and sniff. Instead she turned and trotted off in the other direction, south along the slope, to get a better wind of the hollow before she left for the pine hills.

Straight up-slope from the enemy den she sprang up on a lichened boulder and caught the full wind of the hollow. The desolate yapping of the cubs came to her clearly, but it was the mingle of two scents, many hours old but unmistakable, that startled and gripped her.

One was the blood-chilling smell of the wildcat. The other was the musky scent that the honey-colored vixen had thrown in her extremity.

33

Warily the vixen stole down the hill slope from cover to cover, toward the twenty-foot outcropping that fenced the little hollow in like a rimrock. The fact that she was on enemy ground, and also the strong linger of cat scent, kept her on taut edge, but she slipped on and on till finally she bellied out to the lip of the outcropping and looked down.

Her eyes went briefly to the other vixen's den, a hundred feet out to her left, in the middle of a small mossy flat. It was a poorly chosen burrow, with no concealing brush or dry dirt for a wallow. The four cubs were there. Bewildered and famished, they were wandering around the small flat aimlessly, going in and out of the hole, scratching at their mites, fighting one another, venturing out to the edge of the surrounding deerbush and incessantly calling, calling.

Two of the cubs had the usual tan color of the fox young, but the other two were distinctly more yellowish than their litter mates. Even in the cub-wool phase they showed their heritage from the odd-colored vixen and gave promise of growing into burnished-yellow foxes like her. Though whelped at about the same date as the red vixen's litter, they were livelier and larger than hers had been— large and alert enough to go on short expeditions and begin to learn mouse hunting. Life had run stronger in the young vixen at her first whelping than in the red vixen at the whelping which was near her last, and it was this which had drawn old Carry One to the young mate in the wintry upland woods.

In their hunger the cubs were fighting around over a rabbit skull and a couple of leg bones from a chicken. They were ravenous and their clashes over the dry bones were savage little battles. One of the honey-colored pair, a hair's-width the biggest of the four, was a particularly fearless and determined little tartar. Small as he was, he fought in the unseemly but effective way of an adult fox. He would back up against his litter mates, confuse and blind them with his brush and fuzzy rump, and let them seize a mouthful of his hair. Then he would whirl flash-quick for a strategic slash and bite, and then throw his hind parts into their faces again.

To the right of the red vixen there was a little thicket of spicebush at the foot of the outcropping. In the middle of the thicket the bushes had been torn and the leaves churned up, and there the red vixen saw a lifeless, furry, honey-colored thing, mangled as thoroughly as her own two cubs in the sumac. Evidently the big cat had been lying in ambush on the lip of the rock and had pounced down onto its victim. It could never otherwise have caught the swift, agile vixen. Whether the vixen had been carelessly trotting along the foot of the rock, or trying somehow to defend her young, the torn bushes and roiled leaf bed showed she had put up a desperate fight.

On a smooth, young beech beyond the thicket the wildcat had cleaned its front claws after killing the vixen. The gouges in the beech bark were a good five feet above the ground.

The musky odor that the young vixen had loosed in her death throe set the red vixen trembling anxiously, but then she caught the fresh scent of old Carry One in the woods below and it reassured her. If danger was prowling around in the twilight there, he would cross its nose and draw it away, as he had done unfailingly during their four years together. When she finally located old Carry One, in the undergrowth beyond the mossy flat, she slipped out along the ledge, leaped down and trotted through the brush toward him.

He was in the same restless mood as that afternoon. The constant yapping of the cubs troubled him, but for all his cagey wisdom he was helplessly without answer to their hunger. He could bring prey for a fox family, but he could give it only to the vixen, at a respectful distance. To bring food to a litter of cubs, even when the vixen was dead and the cubs were starving, was completely out of his orbit. He was carrying the remnant of a woodchuck, mostly bones and hide, but he would neither get close to the den or let the cubs straggle anywhere near him.

When the red vixen saw he had food, she flew at him, snapped it up and bolted it. Searching for more food, she went sniffing at the chicken feathers and rabbit fur out along the smooth-padded trail to the flat.

Just inside the brush she stopped and crouched down, watching the enemy vixen's cubs. Her curiosity had mostly been slaked, and she was about to go. After that frightening musky odor and the wildcat's second murderous appearance, neither hunger or usual rounds or anything else had the power to hold her there on Laurel Slope.

The swift April twilight was coming on. The squirrels were back on their den trees and most of the birdcalls had silenced. The major stars were brightening, and a first ghostly hooting drifted down from the rocky hills. As darkness crept into the hollow, the famished cubs were extending their small ventures farther and farther from the den. One of them, wailing along the edge of the brush, caught the scent of the red vixen. It edged up cautiously, saw her, and finally approached her slowly, driven by its gnawing hunger and the smell of her swollen dugs. It sidled around her head and crept toward her flank. But the vixen snarled at it, snapped at it, and it fled, yipping shrilly.

Still the vixen crouched there on the path, her eyes and nose focused now on the cubs, and conscious again of her aching dugs. The sight and scent of warm, fuzzy, hungry cubs seemed to chain her there. The three other cubs had heard the yipping and come over to that side of the flat, and were milling around a few feet from the brush. They too had caught the vixen scent and were sniffing and slavering.

It was the light-colored little fighter that came in first.

He came in boldly, swung around the vixen's head and went for her flank. The vixen snapped at him and nuzzled him away. He bit back at her, growled and came charging in again. That time he seized hold of a nipple before he got rolled. When he came in a third time, he hung on, growling at the vixen through his clenched teeth, even though the vixen by now was making little resistance. Then the others ventured in, one by one, till all four of them were at her, jostling and shoving as they fed. . . .

Many minutes later the red vixen shook them off and stood up. To get away from their importuning, she moved a few steps down the trail. But the cubs followed. They had quit yapping, just as the aching of her dugs had ceased. She heard old Carry One somewhere out in the brush, keeping his distance but circling and guarding. She lifted her muzzle to the night and heard the distant hooting of the upland owls, and she moved on along the path, slowly; realizing dimly the mutual need between herself and the cubs, and yet irrevocably set on starting at once for the wild pine hills.

The cubs stuck to her like burs. When she moved still farther from the mossy flat, not one of them hesitated or whimpered or turned back, but all of them trotted after her eagerly, choosing her instantly over the dank, silent den. They seemed to have the notion that she was taking them on their first hunting expedition and they were all keen for it. The vixen felt her uncertainty leaving her. She had shepherded cubs before, though never cubs quite so small or on so long a trek. Confidently she went on, slowly, with the cubs all around her, under her, brushing against her legs and getting in her way; on and on out along the path and into the night.

SANGAMON SKETCHES

The Lord's Tiny Poultry

ONE spring I began experimenting, more or less haphazardly, at rearing and domesticating wild birds, mostly the small songster species of our yards and gardens. The actual precipitating incident of this business was a violent windstorm, which blew down several trees on my two-acre place and left us with a score of naked little fledglings to pick up and do something about.

In this attempt at raising nestling birds I was in some respects a pioneer and in most respects a complete amateur —rushing in where the experts feared to tread. Sometimes, reading technical papers on young-bird feeding, I wonder how on earth my cut-and-try methods succeeded. For, succeed they did, by and large. In fact, we (myself and my own three fledglings, aged five, seven and eight) had a much larger percentage of successful rearings than obtains in Nature.

Over the course of half a dozen years we maintained a good-sized flock of uniquely tame birds, as genuinely tame as a tiny poultry flock. And we found ourselves with an odd, delightful hobby and fine recreation. It cost us next to nothing; it took us outdoors to sunny fields and green woods; we looked ahead to it each spring with eager zest and later looked back at it with wholly pleasant memories.

As an actual example of the birds we reared, let me tell you about little Jo-dee—her raising, her abiding friendship for us, and the ancient song she sang. I am choosing Jo-dee not because she was one of our prize birds but because she was ordinary and average. Later I'll say a word about those star pets we had, particularly Diana, the star of them all, but to take one of those standouts and play it up as typical would be misleading.

Jo-dee was of quite poor basic material. She wasn't even a native American species but an English sparrow, a song-less, fussy alien. Chiefly for experimental purposes we raised several English sparrows each spring, and among these Jo-dee was considerably above average, but she was not exceptional as a pet. However she illustrates what can be done with poor bird material. For Jo-dee played with us, ate at table with us, lived part of the time in our house, and sang us a song which had not been heard on earth for many thousands of years.

Somebody brought Jo-dee to us when she was just a few hours out of the egg. She got the same treatment as all our fledglings, which meant no flim-flam, bother or routine. Along with a baby redbird, a white-eyed vireo and a song sparrow, she was put into a coffee-can nest on the back porch. Good nests can be made of coconut shells, small flower pots or old strawberry boxes. We used coffee cans merely because we had lots of them. The can was without lid, and the nest was of the open type, like a robin's. The best place to put the can is right on the floor. If a fledgling tumbles out—and tumble they will—nothing but its dignity gets hurt.

Inside, the can should be roughly lined with grass, newspaper or leaves. This is permanent. For the inner lining, which has to be changed, the best material we ever found was plain toilet paper. Make half a dozen laps of this around your fist, pat the end shut, take your fist out, and thus in three seconds you have a nest that's warm, absorbs the moisture, keeps the fledglings dry, and can be renewed very easily.

Different species of fledglings require different foods. For instance, the meat-eaters, like the wrens, take a different diet from the grain-eaters, like the sparrows. But here we're talking about Jo-dee, and all she got was moistened baby-chick mash. Once in a while her nest was changed, and she was lightly dusted every few days with pyrethrum powder to kill mites. We didn't feed Jo-dee every whipstitch as parent birds do. Maybe once an hour, on the average, she got stuffed with mash pellets.

The food that Jo-dee ate, from hatching to flying, may have cost as much as one half of one cent.

On this plain regimen Jo-dee not only thrived; she actually grew faster than if she had been getting the usual food of the wild fledgling. Again and again our test birds were on the wing two or three days ahead of their nest mates.

From the very start Jo-dee was taught to answer a feeding call. This can be a whistle, hiss, a spoon rap against a saucer, but the same call or signal should be used at every feeding so that a fledgling will associate it with food and friendliness. To this call your bird will respond all the rest of its life.

On her chick-mash diet (there are better diets but we didn't know about them then) Jo-dee swiftly sprouted feathers, her bill hardened, and she changed from clumsy egg-shape to the wondrous streamlining of an adult bird. Her wings and tail matured for flight. When she could sit on the nest edge and flutter her wings, she was ready to be taught to fly.

Again, no fuss or bother. She was merely taken out and deposited in a small plum tree, as a protection against cats. There she could hop from twig to twig, learn to balance herself, and make beginning flights of, say, six inches. In that plum tree of ours, during the spring and young summer, you could always see a dozen aerial toddlers getting acquainted with the world and lengthening their flights to a foot, a yard, a nearby lilac.

When somebody appeared with the feeding saucer and called, they would all pile out of the plum tree and come flying with tiny might and main. Some made it to the person, lit on his arm and were fed. Others fell short, on the

grass, and were fed for making the good try. Afterward everybody was deposited in the plum tree again.

For a week after leaving the nest, Jo-dee and the others were kept on the screen porch at night, for safety's sake We perched the gamins on an old laundry rack, and that little congregation surely made an odd sight by flashlight. There they sat in rows, owl-solemn—a weird mixture of baby grosbeaks, yellow warblers, American sparrows, red-birds, blackbirds, bluebirds and whatever else we happened to be raising.

As soon as she could fly well, Jo-dee was encouraged to find her own roosting place, in tree or cornice. But she and all the other tame birds would be on hand at the crack of day, hungry as wolves. Often I worked through the night and went out for a breath of dawn before going to bed. No feeding call was necessary; the squeak of the screen door was the signal for all our flock, titmouse to grackle, to see which one could "git there fustest." The memory of those birds sailing down out of the trees to me is somehow very sweet and unforgettable.

Full-fledged now, little Jo-dee led an ordinary sparrow life. She could fend for herself and mostly she did. But over and above this natural, uncaged existence, she was a true pet. I mean, she stayed with us freely, of her own will. She chirped and fussed around us out in the yard like a tiny bantam hen. She lit on the lawn mower handle when I stopped. She lit on my book when I lay reading and pecked at the print. She was as much a part of the household as any dog, cat, chicken or other domesticated creature could possibly have been.

To square up for the half cent she had cost us, Jo-dee ate weed seeds and worm pests, down in the garden. She paid us back many times over. Some of our native-American pets, like Joe Grackle or Slink Cuckoo, paid us back a hundred times over.

As the summer wore on, Jo-dee developed a personality and little tricks of her own. She liked to have a tug-of-war with you over a bit of colored string—undoubtedly a play preparation for the serious business of nest building. She was fond of hopping around in the sandpile when the neighborhood three-year-olds were digging in it. Not for worlds would they have hurt her. And that goes double and triple for the older children who used our big yards for games and a general hangout. Some of those boys were toughies from across the railroad tracks, but not one of them ever harmed a bird of ours. In fact, anybody caught harming one of those birds would have been cast into the gang's outer darkness.

Children are notoriously fond of pets, and the tame birds of our yard delighted those youngsters more than I can well describe. The miracle of associating with little wild creatures, as they had read of in their books and fairy tales, had there actually come to pass.

In the fall our true migrants left us, for their respective southlands, but the semi-migrants and all-year residents remained. One blizzardy December evening Housekeeper Lucy decided that little Jo-dee ought to be inside that wicked night. That settled it—Jo-dee roosted in the house at night for the rest of the winter! She would appear at the kitchen window in the late afternoon gloom, hop along the sill till someone let her in, then go straight to a window mantel in the dining room and roost.

From this habit developed little Jo-dee's most engaging

trick. By our dinnertime she would be hungry. I would fix food for her on a small wooden plate and then call. She would fly down to the table, sit on the corner at my right and eat. She would eat nearly anything but her preferences were bits of green lettuce, coconut shreds and hard corn-bread. Then, and always in exactly the same way, she would take a drink of water from my spoon, scrape her beak on the edge of her plate and go back to her niche.

The bird that eats at your table differs as much from the shy, furtive bird of the bush as a dog friend differs from a coyote. Constantly Jo-dee and our other pets were giving us glimpses of bird ways which no amount of wildlife observation could ever bring to light. One such glimpse, our discovery that Jo-dee was a fine singer, was downright staggering to us and also to the university ornithologist who studied it.

This discovery, that Jo-dee had a very beautiful little lay, was all the more astonishing because the English sparrow is supposed to have no song whatever, no voice beyond a few harsh notes. Always she sang her lay during the first few minutes after she was let into the house. It was not the sleepy twittering of a bird going to roost, but a true, sustained song—dainty, full of spirals, and as fine as the fragile moon song of the olive-backed thrush.

And this from an English sparrow!

This song of Jo-dee's was no accident. There are no such accidents in Nature. Jo-dee's lay is explained by her ancestry. Songless the English sparrow is now, but once upon a time, far back across the ages, it did sing. It belongs to the finch family, the Fringillidae, which includes some of the best singers in the world. Why singing was abandoned by the English sparrow I don't know, but I do know that under the proper circumstances the song can still be resurrected. With Jo-dee it was a racial memory, a song that came down across the chromosomes of countless generations—a long-forgotten melody of her finch ancestors. Somehow the warmth, light and snugness of our dining room on a blizzardy evening stirred her dim racial memory, and we heard a song which has not been heard on earth since Pleistocene times. . . .

At my first attempts to raise fledglings I went to elaborate pains—eiderdown nests, electric heating pads and other nonsense. I thought fledgling birds were perishable little things. But experience taught me that in many ways they are hardier than a baby chick or turkey. Some of those waifs came to us in very bad shape indeed—starved, frozen, torn by shrike or jay—and yet they pulled through.

In a state of nature fledglings surely need to be hardy. They have to weather heat, cold, rain, sometimes snow; hunger when the food supply fails the parents; and infestation by mites, which kill many young birds and cause the parents to abandon many nests. Besides all this, they are preyed on by cat, weasel, pine squirrel, snake, owl, hawk, crow, jay, shrike, mink and fox.

As you can well imagine, infant mortality among birds

is quite appalling. Only a small fraction of the fledglings hatched out ever live to know the ecstasy of flight. In their life span a pair of birds will produce, say, fifty eggs. On the average *only two* of these will come to maturity and replace the original pair. One chance in twenty-five—that's the odds they are up against.

On the safety of your back porch, with a steady food supply assured, all these natural dangers are eliminated.

The point I'm driving at is this: if you find a fledgling or a nest of them where death genuinely threatens, don't hesitate about taking them home to a coffee-can nest. It's no violation of wildlife ethics to do this. It's a violation not to.

During the nesting season you will come across plenty of fledglings that need you. Just as a person with only book knowledge of wild ginseng can walk through a woods full of it and see hardly any, so it is difficult at first to find these feathered waifs. But with a little experience you will turn up a thoroughly unsuspected number of them. You will look up at a nest, then down at the ground, and see one that has tumbled out. You will spot nests which have been abandoned by the parents, and will learn to recognize the thin, pathetic squeaking of the doomed little things. You will find the runt that has been left behind. You will pick up a tiny thing which a nest-robbing jay has stolen and dropped—as we found our star of stars, Diana. You will find nests where the young simply haven't a chance under the sun. An example of this is the frequently encountered phoebe nest in an old well. On their first flight the young phoebes can't make it to the top; they fall to the water, flutter helplessly and drown. Yet the parent birds go on nesting there year after year.

Concerning the kinds of birds to raise, those with large bills, like the jay, crow and boat-tailed grackle, should be avoided; they have a habit of pecking at bright objects, such as little folks' eyes. Mockingbirds fight other species badly, as do jays and to some extent robins. Fledgling wrens, though exceedingly cute and sleek, are high-strung little bundles and also they are "formula" problems.

Besides the birds above, there are a few odd numbers to avoid for obvious reasons. For example, the water ouzel would require you to have a private cascade. And a tame kingfisher might go exercising his genius in your goldfish bowl.

But a person can't go wrong on any of our splendid American sparrows, such as the white-throat and the vesper. Or our warblers. Or our thrushes, such as the hermit and the bluebird. Or our grosbeaks, redbirds, buntings, juncos, chickadees and other seed-eaters. Or the whole great miscellany of tanagers, orioles, waxwings, swallows, blackbirds, smaller grackles, small woodpeckers, titmice, creepers and kinglets.

I want to emphasize that this fascinating recreation is open to anybody except apartment dwellers in large cities. No special equipment is needed; no big grounds are really necessary. Any sort of postage-stamp back yard is good for a few birds. But how those few can light up the whole summer! How they can make us look ahead in winter to the return of our migrants, the flurry of nest building, the surge of the bursting spring!

The genuine tameness of the coffee-can bird is something a person has to see to appreciate fully. Taming an adult wild bird is a hard, unsatisfactory business. With lots of time, patience and work a wild bird can occasionally be induced to eat from the hand, but this is the exception, and the bird isn't genuinely domesticated then, as I use this term. But if you raise a bird from scratch and it has never known wildness, the little thing will regard you as a natural part of its world and be your lifelong friend.

To think of a bird as a wild creature—and most of us do—is not correct. By nature it is neither wild nor tame, a fact which we proved repeatedly, year after year. The fledgling will take whatever impress is made on it.

A phrase which I once heard a big pious French-Cree use strikes off this whole idea well. We were camped at the east end of Great Slave Lake and were listening to the bird songs in the midnight dusk, out across the sub-Arctic barrens. Ptarmigan were chortling in the willows, and it seemed there was a white-crowned sparrow on every granite swell, sending up its short, silvery song. My companion motioned at the birds. "*La p'tite volaille du bon Dieu,*" he said. Which means, "the Lord's tiny poultry."

That, I think, is the way we should regard our birds— a diminutive sort of poultry which is still in the domain of *le bon Dieu* but which we can tame if we wish, to their gain and ours too. . . .

After you have raised your fledglings you should give them a little simple care, and should extend this to their wild kin also. Every year more and more people are caring for their birds as a recognized part of gracious living. There are several fine books, authoritative and thorough, on bird care, but I will make a few suggestions here.

Birds need water for both drinking and bathing. If you can't find the sort of bath you want at a hardware store or pet shop, a shallow crock with some rocks in it will do. Most baths are too deep. A bird won't bathe in water much deeper than its knees.

City birds need help in regard to their nesting material, especially for the warm lining. Once I bought a dollar's worth of combings at a mattress factory and it was the joy of all the birds in that end of town for several springs.

Birdhouses should be proof against cats. More boxes for hole nesters, like the woodpecker, bluebird and nuthatch, should be put up. Wren houses should be in partial shade. If they are exposed to the full sun, as so sadly many of them are, the inside gets so stifling on a hot day that the wrenlets struggle around, finally fall out on the ground and perish.

For the meat-eaters, two pounds of beef suet in an orange bag, so hung that squirrels and cats can't get at it, is the best wrinkle I know of. It's astonishing how long this will last, though it has dozens of visitors daily. I always have several of these around my place. For the seed-eaters, baby-chick scratch grain is a safe, good and inexpensive food. Certain foods, such as rice, should not be used. Several small feeding stations are usually better than one, to prevent monopolizing.

One thing—if you start feeding birds during the cold months, don't do it in on-again, off-again fashion. See to it that they have an ample supply of food every day without fail. Else, don't start feeding them at all. Many of our semi-migrants are attracted to feeding stations in the late fall and will stay throughout the winter, several hundred miles north of their normal winter habitats. Because of their high pulse rate, body temperature and other factors, birds use up energy fast and they can't get along without food for even a single day in severe weather. If their feeding station fails them, especially during conditions of snow or icing when they can't get at seeds or other food, they will weaken and perish in just a day or two.

One bitter, murky February evening I had a flock of several hundred native sparrows—tree, field, even a few chipping sparrows among them—come drifting weakly in to my feeding station. It was a pitiful sight. Many fell in the snow and died within a few minutes. We took scores of others inside and tried to resuscitate them but they were too far gone. This particular flock, I feel sure, had been depending on a certain big, ornate feeding station about half a mile away, but the owner had gone off and the remaining food supply had been blanketed by a new fall of snow.

Another kindness we can do our birds is to furnish them with a dust bath. Yet, you rarely see one of these. A bird bathes in dust to get rid of its mites, of which hundreds of species are known. They kill many birds outright and weaken a great many more. There is little if any natural dust in winter. The long rainy spells in spring cause a high mortality among birds not by bringing on pneumonia epidemics, as was formerly thought, but by destroying the dust wallows and so allowing the mite plague to grow unchecked. Almost any kind of very fine and dry material, even road dust, will do. Mix a little pyrethrum powder (never DDT) with it.

The cost of rearing a flock of fledglings and caring for all your tiny poultry throughout the year needn't exceed the price of a good mashie or an evening at the theater. If you can raise only a few tame birds, you still are doing your bit toward building back one of our tremendous natural assets.

The person who wishes to take up bird rearing as a hobby should read up on this subject—without letting the experts discourage him too much—and then should begin modestly, with just a few fledglings of some hardy species. The English sparrow is one of our hardiest and best birds for this purpose and it is everywhere available. In the business of feeding and rearing fledglings there is a great deal of know-how and "feel," and only actual experience can teach a person these.

The dollar-and-cents value of our birds is just too big a topic to be more than mentioned here. When authorities tell us that *one* cuckoo will clean out five hundred nests of tent caterpillars in a summer; that *one* brown creeper is "worth five bushels of apples" in anybody's orchard; that *one* single species, the field sparrow, in one single state, Iowa, destroys nearly a thousand *tons* of ragweed seeds in a year—well, these items give a few flitting glimpses of the picture. Constantly our birds are fighting our battle against the insect world. Now and then we read prophecies that some day the insect powers will whip us in a struggle for the earth. While alarums like these are rather silly, it nevertheless is a fact that our constant and growing battle with the insect myrmidons would be astronomically costly without our birds to help us. . . .

Some of the birds we raised deserted us flatly. Some of them that were migrants didn't show up again in the spring. Others, we suspected, hung around mostly for the grub. But the majority gave us an abiding friendship. The exceptionally fine ones stand out vividly in memory. There was Blue Robin, our gentle bluebird. And Cheery, the yellow warbler. And Slink Cuckoo, the rain crow, sounding his ventriloquial *kow-kow-kow* as he cleaned out a nest of webworms. And Frank Oriole, who turned out to be Frances Oriole. And our splendid scarlet tanager, Drake—a flame-colored jewel in the greenery. All these were definitely better pets than little Jo-dee, and incomparably better than any caged "pet" in its little wire Sing Sing.

But still higher stood our Big Three—Joe, Johnny and Diana. How I would like to tell you at length about Joe Grackle—lovable, clowny, waddling, unsquelchable Joe! He could sing no better than a rusty hinge but he was eternally trying. He went along on some of our country trips, but usually he got lost and came home by himself.

Or about Johnny Chuck-a-Lear, our redbird, whose fine, buoyant whistle in the gloom of the Illinois winter was a reminder that courage and optimism are precious qualities. He was in and out of the house as though he owned it. He let me firm up his poorly built nest and even dust his fledglings without a trace of fear, though his dun wife was a wild bird and wanted nothing to do with us.

And lastly, Diana, star of the Big Three, star of all the birds we ever raised . . . One day myself and a lady friend, the Wanderer, were walking in a field and I was trying, without much success, to persuade the Wanderer that the responsibilities of being stepmother to three small girls would not be without recompense and would not interfere too much with her career as poet and novelist. In the midst of our talk we came upon a fledgling so small that we couldn't identify it. Plucked from the nest by a robber jay, it bore a bad wound and also it was bruised from being dropped. It showed gameness under the cruel bite of our pocket-kit antiseptic, and it went home in the

Wanderer's lace kerchief to a special seashell nest on my desk.

I had to go north on a lengthy trip, leaving home and girls in the Wanderer's charge, but reports about the fledgling followed me by letter. From the very start, I heard, Diana was a lady. She ate daintily, the Wanderer wrote, and she preened her first pinfeather the instant it appeared. The puzzle about her species was cleared up one day by a wireless to me:

"Diana is a waxwing!"

This was great news, fully justifying a radiogram. In my opinion—and many ornithologists think likewise—the satiny elegance and exquisite coloring of the cedar waxwing make it the prettiest bird in America, though others may be brighter, gaudier. The waxwing's bohemian ways, its polite habit of passing food to its neighbor, and its other graces have endeared it to bird-loving people ever since Audubon.

When I got back home and we raised Diana, she lived up to the waxwing's reputation for unpredictability. We never knew what to expect of the shiny creature. One night she would roost in my study, behind a bust of Keats. The next night, like as not, she would spend with the Wanderer, in the latter's apartment five blocks away. All during the summer, fall and winter she would go away and stay for days at a time. We forgave her this, knowing she was torn between affection for us, her foster kin, and a thirst to be gadding about with her bohemian, Greenwich-Village

kind. When she perched on your sleeve and spoke the lisping flight-word of the waxwing, you felt she was asking
you to leave your work and go flying off with her to the
wild hills.

When spring came, the Wanderer departed from the
Midwest, but Diana stayed with us. We never saw her
mate, and her marriage must have been a loose tie, but at
cherry time she built a nest in a small live oak and reluc-
tantly took up the brooding of her daintily purpled eggs.
Perhaps I imagined it but when I stood on the stepladder
to talk a minute with her, she seemed to wear a look of
boredom and of distaste with being "tied down."

But she did successfully hatch and mother a brood. I
wrote about this domesticity to the Wanderer in Paris,
pointing out that even Diana had given in to the great
norms of life—home, children and settled ways. But the
argument, alas, fell among stones. And finally Diana too
departed. But to this day the faint lisping note of waxwings in the sky reminds me of slim elegance and a restless heart, and may they both be happy, wherever they
may be.

The Mystery of the Big Hop

FOR several years after I began doing what my university friends referred to somewhat tolerantly as "collecting rabbit tracks," I was puzzled no end by certain huge cottontail leaps which I occasionally saw in the snow. We were living then outside of town, in a wildish section of scrub farm land and sassafras hills where rabbits were plentiful, and my "collection" of their tracks grew apace with each fresh snowfall.

These huge leaps I saw every now and then were comparable to coming across the trail of a man who had been walking along at an ordinary stride but occasionally had taken three or four gargantuan steps of twenty-five or thirty feet each.

Though I didn't see these tremendous rabbit jumps very often, I did run onto them enough to know that they were a part of a rabbit's routine and not merely some freakish business. Just as definitely they were none of the half-dozen kinds of rabbit hops and leaps I was familiar with but were something very special.

In just hopping around to feed or play, a rabbit covers

only from one to three feet per hop. In its first burst of
speed when flushed from its form, it averages four or five
feet per jump. In full, straightaway flight, to escape a fox
or coyote, it will do six to eight feet per leap, with an absolute top (in my records, at least) of nine feet. But these
huge leaps ranged from twelve feet to fifteen! Furthermore, they seemed entirely without rhyme or reason. In
the snow I'd see where a cottontail had been hopping along
ordinarily, then suddenly had taken three or four of these
huge jumps, then back to ordinary again.

In my field notes, chiefly about rabbit feeding habits and
the home range of individuals, I had the explanation of
the big hop all the time, in the form of scattered clues, but
somehow I hadn't put these clues together. Reading snow
trails correctly and understanding them can be a recondite
business.

To the knowing eye an animal's snow trail can tell quite
a story, and often it yields information obtainable in no
other way. For instance, the habits of the rare pekan or
fisher are known very largely from its record in the snow.
To be sure, some trails, like the deer's or the skunk's, are
not too informative and may be monotonous, but others
are so engrossing that you'll follow them for miles. Of our
common animals the weasel and fox are, to me, the most
interesting to snow-trail and study. But the cottontail is
high on the list, and some surprising new knowledge about
this odd, likeable creature has come from its snow record.

By this record you'll discover that the home range of a

rabbit is astonishingly small. Give it a den-shelter against vile weather, and a dense covert or two against the sudden swoop of enemies, and it will live its whole life contentedly within an acre or so, especially if its range touches that of another rabbit, with which it can play. You'll discover that it's not a creature of the deep night, as commonly supposed, but of the two twilights, evening and dawn. True, when the moon rides high it does cavort all night, mostly going through its queer, intricate, little-known play maneuvers with other rabbits; but during pitch-dark times it runs little if any. You'll also learn that it's an abstemious eater and can get along fine on a moiety of coarse, unpalatable food which most other nibblers and browsers would turn up their noses at. While it prefers those plants which stay green all winter, it readily eats bark, dry grass, twig ends, pine needles and suchlike, and a frozen apple is a feast for it.

Most of the complaints about rabbit depredations in orchards and gardens are ill-founded. For county agents and others I have many times investigated these complaints, and four times out of five the damage is referable to the groundhog or to meadow mice (*Microtus*). As stated, a rabbit eats very sparingly—a couple of ounces in the evening and a couple in the morning. Pound for pound a groundhog eats approximately *twenty-five times* as much as a rabbit.

Contrary to popular belief, especially among hunters, a rabbit does not run its fastest uphill but on the level.

However, it does *seem* to run fastest uphill because there it outdistances a dog or fox more easily than on the flat.

As for its enemies of the winter night, the list is so formidable that a person wonders how the cottontail ever manages to survive at all. The weasel, cat, owl, fox, coyote, lynx, bobcat, wolf and still others hunt it continually and with great skill, yet the rabbit not only holds its own against them but spends most of its time in play! The snow record explains its success. After a bit of study, you'll begin to recognize the rigid safety patterns of a rabbit's movements when it feeds or plays. An invisible tether of instinct keeps it from getting too far away from a hole or covert. That is just one example, and a rather simple one, of these complex safety patterns.

Occasionally, it's true, you do see where a rabbit trail ends with tragic abruptness in a few flecks of blood and the telltale sweep of big pinions on the snow, or in a few draggles of fur where an ambushed fox scooped up a cottontail, gave it a quick brain-bite and lugged it off. But for every one of these sad little tableaux, you will see dozens of encounters where the rabbit's safety habits kept it from harm.

You hear it said all the time that a rabbit is a timid, furtive animal. Now I wonder about that. You'll see one of these places in the snow where a fox or owl missed a rabbit by inches, and a few hops farther on that rabbit starts nibbling on a crabapple twig. That doesn't seem to me any sign of a timid, cowardly nature. The rabbit just isn't a fighting animal. All its instincts are geared to fleeing and escaping, and death hovers over it so constantly that it takes danger in quite a nonchalant manner.

In the midst of all these familiar snow recordings, there was that unexplained big hop. I knew it was no sort of feeding, flight or scare jump. Nor was it a "spy hop"— where an animal leaps up high to see over vegetation— because the huge leaps often occurred in little open areas where spy hops weren't in order. And from my observations of rabbit play, I was fairly sure it had no connection with that.

Then, one brilliant winter night, I saw a cottontail, in fact two of them, actually making this tremendous leap and under circumstances which explained it instantly.

During the fall of that particular year three wild rabbits, living in a brushy little grove at the edge of our yard, had been coming out at twilight and cavorting around on a level terrace outside my study window. With a few tiles and a box I built them a fine, dry shelter-den just inside the grove, and they took to it thankfully when winter came on. Tom, Dick and Harry I called them. But one day in early February the younger generation, now verging toward high school, informed me that as a Nature observer I wasn't as bright as I thought I was; that those rabbit names should be Tom, Dick and *Mary*.

On the night in question a large cottontail stranger appeared on the terrace. I found out later, by tracking him, that his home range was a little clump of pines four hundred yards away—a far distance indeed for a rabbit to journey.

For a while after the stranger appeared, Tom and Dick confined themselves to stamping their feet at him, as buck rabbits do. No doubt they were telling him that they'd butt his brains out if he didn't go back where he belonged. But the stranger paid no attention to them. His interest

centered on Mary, nibbling a cabbage head which I'd staked up in the middle of the terrace.

Then, as I watched, I saw Tom take a quick little run, somewhat like the approach run of a broad-jumper, and go sailing through the air on one of those tremendous leaps. And then another leap, this one arching high up over Mary and the cabbage head.

Immediately the stranger cottontail set out to show what *he* could do along that line. He took the momentum run and gave *three* leaps, even more tremendous than

Tom's. Those three leaps carried him nearly all the way across that fifty-foot terrace. Twice more this strange performance was repeated, the two buck rabbits hopping around and across that terrace like two outlandish Mexican jumping beans.

Well, there it was, at long last, and no doubt about it. A "show off" hop. A part of the rabbit mating ritual. A display of male prowess, in rabbit terms. Evidently in the eyes of a doe cottontail the ability to hop big is a very impressive point.

When I went to my notes and examined them, I saw that all my records of the puzzling, oversized leaps occurred in February or March, the mating season coincident with snow, and that these leaps occurred only when one or more rabbits were around to watch the jumper.

Clearly the cottontail stranger out-hopped Tom—and presumably Dick too—and by all the rules of the game he should have taken over, the winnah, while Tom and Dick retreated to the far corner of the grove and gnashed their teeth. But it didn't work out that way, and don't ask me why. A good many of those pat rules and sayings about the outdoors and its creatures don't hold water too well. Anyhow, as I discovered by the snow-trail story the next morning, the cottontail stranger left soon after the exhibition of big-hopping and returned to his home pine thicket. Once again it was Tom, Dick and Mary playing around and consorting together on the moonlit terrace.

Mushroom Hunting

Y OU, pheasant hunter, tramping through the woods and sunny fields of autumn—when you happen upon one of those white, pumpkin-like oddities which some people call puffballs and others call "melons of the moon," don't for goodness sake haul off with your boot and kick it to smithereens, as foolish hunters usually do. Though you get no pheasant or even so much as roust a cottontail, your day is made. Pluck that "moon melon" and take it tenderly along home, and you'll have plenty to show for your hours afield. You'll have a delicious meal, or several meals, of food you'll swear is better than the game you didn't get.

And you, trout fisherman, at apple-blossom time—when you come upon a spawning of those curious growths-of-the-earth which look like a cross between a corncob and a sponge, don't mutter "toadstools" and walk indifferently by. You'll be passing up something far more rare and special than the golden trout of the high Cascades. Something that would cost you as much as twenty-five dollars per serving—when you can get it at all—at expensive restaurants in New York or Paris. The knowledgeable gourmet speaks of the morel mushroom reverently as the "finest dish on earth."

And you, Farmer Dell's wife—when you look out upon your pasture some dewy September morn and see that overnight it has been sprinkled white with the buttons and elfin umbrellas of *Agaricus campestris*, in magic fairy rings and beds of no man's sowing, hurry out there and start picking or your cows will pounce on them and gobble them all up. Or they'll be eaten by woodchucks, rabbits, meadow mice, crickets, and the host of other creatures that know a toothsome morsel when they see it. The identical mushroom that costs you at least half a dollar a pound at the grocery—out there you can gather bushels of it for free.

"Who—me?" some souls may say. "Catch me gathering wild mushrooms! Why, people get poisoned doing that. No sir*eeee*, not me."

Fiddlesticks. The ordinary person exercising ordinary common sense can gather mushrooms afield with perfect safety, as indeed several millions of folk do, year after year. Those few people who get into trouble—and they are very few, statistics-wise—are the fools and nitwits who'd get into trouble whatever they did. We don't let the idiots of the highway or the occasional rifle-armed moron of the deer woods keep us from driving a car or hunting, and no more should we allow their foolish cousins to keep us from the enjoyable outdoors recreation of mushroom gathering.

The mushroom hunter never comes back empty-handed
—well, *almost* never. He needs no costly paraphernalia,
only a dime-store basket and a kitchen knife. Throughout
the open season, from young April till long after hickory-
nutting time, he never lacks an excuse for an outdoors
jaunt. Nor does he perjure his soul by telling lies about the
big puffball that got away—though I must admit that
mushroom hunters have their own special brands of pre-
varication and also resort to some fancy skulduggery
against one another on occasions.

The way to become a mushroom hunter is to start with
just one kind, the kind I shall tell you about in a minute,
and then gradually add other species till you have a repertoire of about half a dozen. There are hundreds of edible
mushrooms, plus scores that are inedible because they are
leathery, woodlike or bad tasting, plus some eleven or
twelve that are moderately poisonous, and one (the Destroying Angel) that is very poisonous. Learning this whole
field would be a laborious job, and it's entirely unnecessary. There are four species which are so abundant and so
well spread out over the season that they are all you need
to begin with, and each of these four kinds has some feature so distinctive that identification is easy and simple.

As a matter of fact, the "Big Four" among mushrooms,
the four I am going to talk about here, make up the bulk
of the mushrooms gathered by the expert hunters.

Let me say, emphatically, that all those amateur rules,
such as the silver spoon test, for distinguishing poisonous

and nonpoisonous mushrooms are completely unreliable and dangerous and must be shunned. The one and only safe method is to know each species you gather, know its name, its distinctive features, and be able to tell it from any other species.

The puffball is by all means the mushroom you should start with. These white, roundish, conspicuous objects, some a bit flattened like a Kentucky pumpkin, others pear-shaped, others as round as a basketball, can't possibly be mistaken for any other mushroom. In fact, they're like nothing else outdoors. The different species range from marble size to as big as a half-bushel basket. Because the small ones are hard to peel and sometimes grow on media which give them a poor flavor, I myself gather only those as large as an apple or larger and I recommend that you do the same. These larger varieties always taste excellent.

The one rule we need to know about puffballs is simple and infallible: *If it's white all the way through, eat it.* When the spores inside a puffball begin to ripen, the "meat" turns brownish, and though it is not poisonous it tastes bitter. Incidentally, a puffball will remain fresh in the icebox for several days and often you find a *Calvatia* so big that it takes you that long to eat it up.

In preparing a puffball, remove the rind or peridium, which is about orange-peel thick, and then slice the meat with a sharp knife, as you would slice a dish of mush. Frying is the traditional way of cooking puffballs, and the fried slabs are so delicious that most people never go on to any other way, but diced puffball goes fine in soups, stews and gravies. It's a little too delicate in flavor to make good sauces.

The larger puffballs come on in the late summer—mid-August in the central Illinois latitude—and their season extends to the first hard freeze. You can go back and gather them at the same place year after year. The *Calvatia* puffballs, which include the big boys, often grow in fairy rings, and truly a fairy ring of these large moon melons is a spectacular sight and a prize find. In communities where a number of mushroom hunters operate, the location of these rings is of course well known and the competition to grab off the "melons" as soon as they reach respectable size leads to all sorts of chicanery and artful dodges.

One time, scouting out a fairy ring which was notorious for the big ones it produced, I found nine baby giants about the size of grapefruit. Being in competition for that patch with a doctor, a minister, a professor and a couple of other unscrupulous characters, I covered up seven of the nine with brush and leaves, as carefully as a hen turkey conceals her clutch. The two which I left open, to disarm suspicion, apparently disappeared the next day. My own seven grew monstrously, and when I finally took them home I invited my rivals to drop by and see them and have some convulsions of envy. My doctor friend said, "No, you come and see what *I've* got." When I went over I found him the proud possessor of a *Calvatia gigantea* that nudged the world record —a puffball measuring twenty-five and a half inches in diameter! Unknown to me, he had found and concealed those two decoys, which I hadn't regarded as promising, and one of them had grown into the whopper.

The giant puffball is the largest fungus on earth. But its spores are among the tiniest of seeds, if we may call them that. A *gigantea* eighteen inches in diameter will contain *six trillion* spores.

Exceedingly tiny and light, mushroom spores are equipped with dainty flutes and vanes to catch the slightest stir of air. Sucked up by rising currents, they ascend to great heights and ride the stratospheric winds all around the world. Once I inveigled an Army pilot to take me up into the wild blue yonder and with a crude grease board I trapped spores at twenty thousand feet. Since then they have been found at twice that height. This dissemination by the intercontinental winds is the reason why mushrooms are pretty much the same earthwide, at the same latitude and under the same conditions. The chanterelle or the slender galera that you find in your back yard may have originated in Kashmir or a valley of the Carpathians.

So much for the puffball. Stick to the larger sizes and remember that one simple rule—*white all the way through*—and you can't possibly make a mistake.

*   *   *

As already mentioned, the pasture mushroom is the identical species, *Agaricus campestris,* which is grown commercially, and so you can learn this mushroom simply by buying a few at the grocery and studying them. Buy specimens at different stages of development. Notice that in the button stage the gills are covered by the "veil."

At the next step, when the veil has been broken, notice the pinkish color of the gills. Because of this distinctive feature the majority of people call this mushroom the "pink-gill." As the cap expands till it is nearly flat, the spores ripen, the gills turn dark, and at maturity they are a pastel black, with a tinge of purple.

Being a fungus, a mushroom does not need sunlight,

as chlorophyll plants do, and so *A. campestris* is grown mostly in caves and other underground situations where the temperature and moisture can be kept at optimum. It is harvested in the button stage partly because it stays salable longer that way and partly because customers are said to prefer it that way. But I myself think the flavor of *campestris* is much better when the cap is about three quarters expanded and the gills are starting to darken, and most of my fellow hunters seem to agree on this point.

Making spore prints of mushrooms is quite an interesting business and you should try it some time, whether you're a mushroom fan or not. It's so simple that any six-year-old can do it; in fact, children will spend many fascinated hours making these prints and building up a collection. For a spore print any gill-type mushroom will do. Merely break off the stem, lay the cap on a piece of paper with the gills down, and place over it a drinking glass, cup or suchlike, to prevent any stir or movement of air inside. In the course of three or four hours the spores will fall down onto the paper and make a perfect facsimile of the gills, to the minutest detail and in the particular color of that species. By gently blowing fixative or some clear plastic over the print, it can be preserved indefinitely.

Spore-print colors can only be described as lovely. Soft, pastel hues, ranging from gossamer white through amethysts, lilacs, yellows and purples to ebony black, they are like no other colors you ever see. Some mushroom keys are based on spore-print colors, and so this is one means of easy identification.

More people gather the "pink-gill" than any other kind. It has several relatives, others of the *Agaricus* family, which are found in the woods, but *campestris* occurs mostly in the open—pastures, lawns, golf courses and along the roadside—from July till late October, and in good years it grows abundantly indeed. It is not unusual to gather a bushel of them within a couple of acres.

Whenever your cookbook says "mushrooms" it means the pink-gill. So you can look there and find the different ways of using *campestris*. This mushroom is quite versatile and can be used for soups, gravies, sauces and stews, besides frying.

Now we come to that mushroom masterpiece, that delight supreme of the gourmet, that visitor at apple-blossom time—the morel. To the scientist it is *Morchella conica* (or *M. esculenta*); to foolish souls it's a toadstool; to our pioneer forefathers and to many people today it's the "sponge mushroom," and to everybody who eats it, it's the last word in foods. You don't have to get used to it or acquire the taste, as with raw oysters or green olives. With the first morsel of it you're hooked.

Take a good look at a picture of the morel and you'll recognize it instantly afield. It has not one but several distinctive features. Notice that it has no gills. The spores are borne in little sac processes called *asci*, which are distrib-

uted all over the surface and are microscopic in size. Notice the elongated, conelike form of the cap. Note the
broad, irregularly shaped pits of the surface and also the
network of narrow ridges which run more or less up and
down. When you pick one, notice that the stem and the
cap, both equally good to eat, are hollow. Altogether, no
other mushroom looks anything like it.

Alas, the morel season is brief. In the latitude of central Illinois you find the earliest ones, perhaps no bigger
than a thimble, around mid-April, and by the first of June
they are all gone. When the first apple bloom appears,
start looking, so you'll miss none. The height of the season
is reached when the warblers are passing through, or just
a few days later. You look up and see a gorgeous little
Blackburnian flashing around among the pink and white
of the apple blossoms, and you look down and see a morel
in the young grass or pushing up through a drift of last
autumn's leaves. If you live within driving distance of
high hills or mountains, where the march of spring will
be maybe a fortnight later than in the valleys, you can
extend the morel season a bit, but otherwise resign yourself to the fact that about four weeks each year is all the
good morel hunting you will have.

Like gold, morels are where you find 'em; there seems
to be little rhyme or reason about their occurrence. They
are "repeaters"; that is, they are found at the same place
for two, three or four successive seasons. But beyond that
I don't know of any rules that hold water. Morels occur

in the deepest woods and in wide-open fields; in black muck soil and in acidy clay, and in greatly differing habitats. I have found them growing among the bulrushes of soggy swamps, and high up on Mount Washington in patches of wintergreen. Old apple orchards are reputed to be the best hunting grounds for them, but I've combed many an old orchard and found none, then stepped over into an adjacent field or woods and found plenty.

One thing, you're not apt to find morels, or any other mushrooms, in orchards, woods or fields that have been sprayed. Certain salts in the commonly used sprays, especially copper salts, are deadly to most fungi, and the least trace of these spray residues in the soil or the wood host will prevent mushrooms from growing. I have noted this complete absence of mushrooms in old groves that haven't been sprayed for the last thirty years.

According to all accounts, the morel crop has been steadily and emphatically growing during the last decade or two. A generation ago a gallon of morels was a very good haul for half a day's hunting. Now you can often gather literally a peck of them under one tree. The explanation of this is simple—the elm blight factor. Morels grow on the lateral roots of elms that are dead or dying, and grow profusely there. The time range seems to be from a year before the tree actually succumbs to about three years afterward. So, visit dead elms in the morel season. A couple of good trees and you can go back home with a basketful.

In recent years some surprising discoveries have been made about mushrooms as food, and research now in progress may turn up facts even more surprising. It used to be thought that mushrooms were merely a tasty flavorizer for various dishes. But then the food value of mushrooms was studied, and it was found that besides their minerals and other nutritional factors many species contain a considerable percentage of protein, of a very good kind. This protein is the reason why a meal of mushrooms "satisfies" a person, like a meal of meat. Then the nutritional chemists discovered in mushrooms a battery of four invaluable enzymes, in the nature of tenderizers and digestants. Consequently mushrooms were recommended for certain invalid diets, and the results have been generally good.

But now one line of research is digging still deeper—into the possibility that mushrooms may contain certain substances of an antibiotic nature. In various folklores and "native medicine" practices, mushrooms have long been held to be helpful or even curative with certain diseases. Before we dismiss this as witch-doctor stuff we should remember that mushrooms are closely akin to, and sometimes grow in symbiotic association with, those molds and soil fungi which are the source of penicillin, the different "mycins" and others of our "wonder drugs." We should remember also that folklore in several European countries had it that a poultice of moldy bread was good for external infections and that pellets of moldy bread were good for internal infections. In pre-penicillin days a few doctors, here and abroad, surreptitiously tried out this home remedy by giving moldy-bread pills to critically ill patients, and they saved lives by it. But they didn't know why the remedy worked and they were afraid of getting laughed at if they publicly told of their results, so penicillin had to wait till Fleming discovered it properly.

In China and India, mushroom broth has been used for many centuries against fever diseases of the typhoid type. At a Calcutta hospital a team of British medical scientists investigated this and their results were so excellent that now a standardized broth taken orally and also a hypodermic injection are being used as regular procedure.

In view of all this, it could be that some startling secrets lie hidden in the rather extensive folklore about mushrooms. Anyhow, let's hope so. If my doctor should some time tell me that I had stomach trouble and I could get well by eating plenty of mushrooms—well, I could face up to the situation philosophically. Especially if he would specify morels.

The last of our Big Four is the oystershell, so called because of its shape. Many people, including most of the textbooks, call this simply the oyster mushroom, because that's what it tastes like. Others call it the woods oyster, because that's where you mostly find it. Scientists call it *Pleurotus ostreatus*.

With mushroom hunters the oystershell is Old Dependable. It's a repeater; the same log or stump will produce a fresh crop every twenty days or so all summer, and will keep on doing this for two or three years. It is one of the most prolific of mushrooms. And its season is the longest of all, beginning in early April and lasting till December. In fact you can gather oystershells in the dead of winter. When you find a cluster of them that have dried up and are bone hard, simply brush off the snow and ice, take them home, put them in water for an hour or so, and they will swell up to natural size and be quite edible.

Ostreatus is one of the easiest mushrooms to recognize. In the first place it grows only on wood—an old stump, a fallen trunk, a dead branch or pocket of a live tree. The shape of the cap varies but typically it reminds one of an oyster half-shell. The stem is not attached to the center of the cap, as with the pasture and most other mushrooms, but laterally—to one side. The caps are light gray to brownish gray; the spore print is white or pale lilac. Usually *ostreatus* grows in clusters, the caps thickly crowded and overlapping like shingles, and sometimes one cluster will weigh as much as two pounds.

But the unique and distinctive feature about the oyster-shell is the fact that the gills *run down onto the stem*. This feature is called decurrent gills, and it's an unmistakable means of identification. When you find a mushroom growing on wood and with gills running down onto the stem, it's an oystershell; it can't possibly be anything else.

Many trees—apple, maple, elm, ash and others—are host

to *ostreatus* but it never grows on their living wood. Its mycelium, or what we might call its root system, is a mass of whitish threads, which penetrate the dead wood and extract nutriment from it. Like many other mushrooms, *ostreatus* buds during the coolish spells in summer, when the temperature dips into the 60's for a day or two. When the weather warms again, these buds grow into the fruit caps.

When you find oystershells, remember the place. You can harvest them there seven or eight times during the summer. It's not unusual to gather five pounds from a log at one picking. I once gathered thirty-seven pounds from an elm log at one time, and once during an entire season a large maple stump in my yard yielded one hundred twenty-six pounds. That's what I mean when I say the oystershell is prolific.

Here is a wrinkle—and a dandy one—you can work with *ostreatus*. If you find a log growing them, a log of a size you can handle, bring it home with you, put it in the back yard and wet it with a hose every few days. It will bear just as well there as where you found it. Each fall I bring in a couple or three oystershell logs and put them in the basement, and when the blizzards blow I eat fresh mushrooms.

Because it is clean to grow—no manure compost—and the yields are so large, *ostreatus* is raised commercially in Europe, notably Hungary, and in Japan, where it is grown on big racks of logs. The famous Shiitake mushroom which the Japanese ship all over the world is nothing but the oystershell.

In Nature's scheme of things the appointed work of the fungus legions is to keep the earth clean and fresh. Consider what happens when a tree, a maple let's say, dies. The oystershell starts working on it and continues for two or three years—till it has exhausted its particular food substances. Then some other mushroom takes over and "reduces" the dead wood further. This process may be repeated three or four times, each successive mushroom being lower in the fungus scale, till at last the log is nothing more than crumbly rot. Then the molds and slimes take over and reduce the log to black, rich humus.

If it were not for this activity of the fungi, trees and plants would die, fall over and persist for decades or even centuries. Soon the surface of the earth would be a piled-up mass of dead vegetation, impossible to traverse, subject to great fires and blanketing any new growth. You get a faint glimpse of this sort of thing at certain places in the Canadian sub-Arctic, where I have collected fungi. There you will sometimes find deep valleys where the windfall has piled up to a depth of thirty or forty feet because the wood-destroying fungi are mostly of the shelf variety and very slow in growing.

Besides the mushroom Big Four, which the beginner can gather with complete safety, there are of course dozens of other kinds, such as the corals, the fine-flavored clitocybes, the coprinuses, the big, snow-white hedgehog, the fawn-colored pluteus. All these and many others are very common; you see them everywhere. Estimates have been made of the amount of edible mushrooms which go to waste each year country-wide, and these estimates are quite staggering. Far exceeding any single crop we grow, the total runs into millions of tons.

Some time we will get around to utilizing this excellent and abundant food. In the meanwhile you and I can spend a summer hour outdoors and come back with a basketful.

NORTHLAND TRAILS

The Battle of Red Rock Bluff

THERE was a temporary lull in the grim struggle across on the bluff. The big rogue bear, intent on getting at the two wolf dens out near the point of the butte, had dropped the battle for the moment and was out of sight in a little snow *couloir*, cooling himself off, no doubt, and licking the slashes that the wolves had given him.

The eight adult wolves that had survived the first round of their stouthearted defense of the two dens and the two litters of cubs had flung themselves down on a patch of old snow, in a scatter of dwarf junipers between the dens and the *couloir*, and were waiting for the bear to come out and break open the fight again.

I suggested to Joe, as we crouched in our nest of rocks and watched, that maybe the grizzly had had enough and now would go on about its business. But the Indian grunted, "*Nu-numwach,*" which is the Cree way of saying an emphatic no. When a bear, especially a surly old rogue, takes a hanker for something, Joe said, it's the pigheadedest animal in the mountains. That grizzly, he said, had smelled or seen the two litters of plump little cubs playing around outside the dens and was sot on making a dinner of them, and nothing short of an earthquake stick (dynamite) could knock that idea out of its skull.

Stark and bright under the clear mountain sun, the high, red-rock bluff, over across a deep, spruce-dark gorge, was only about two hundred yards from us and slightly lower than our position. With my binoculars I had drawn the dens and battleground up close and could see everything over there in good detail . . . The two dead wolves that had been caught, ripped and killed by a swipe of the grizzly's terrible claws. The other wolves on the snow patch, their tongues lolling out, their flanks heaving. And out near the north edge of the butte the two dens, with some marmot skins, rabbit fur, a bighorn skull and some bones around them.

The side-by-side burrows, in a clay hardpan, were mere shallow pockets that the bear could dig out with a few scoops once it got through the wolf defenders.

Now and then, at the dark openings, I caught a glimpse of fuzzy little heads and sharp little ears. But the cubs instinctively knew that death was on the prowl around there, in the heavy, musky bear smell, and except for quick, frightened peeks they were cowering as far back in the burrows as they could get.

The two neighboring dens, almost a duplex arrangement, and the Scotch dozen of adult wolves over there, were more or less typical of the small wolf "colonies" you find in the northern Rockies and elsewhere. Wolves are extremely sociable creatures. The lone wolf you read so much about is rare indeed in the wild. A wolf which for any reason loses its litter mates and other kin will abandon its home range, start traveling and hardly stop to sleep or even hunt enough to quiet its stomach gnaw till it finds other wolves that will allow it to throw in with them.

Besides the cubs and their parents, the little colony over on the butte may have contained grandparents, uncles, cousins and still others, loosely affiliated but all intensely loyal and cooperative. The only limiting factor in these wolf communities is the amount of game within hunting radius. Out on the Great Barrens, where the summertime supply of rabbit, lemming, caribou and moulting water-fowl is nearly unlimited, colonies of forty or fifty adults and half a dozen litters of cubs are not at all uncommon.

I myself hadn't seen the first phase of the battle be-tween the wolves and the meat-hungry bear. I'd been down the mountainside in some windfall, collecting sub-Arctic fungi for a university botany department, and Joe had come partway down and summoned me. But the battleground area, a hundred feet from the dens, where the two wolves lay dead and the heather, sedge and foot-high birches were all torn up and trampled, showed how valiant a fight the wolves had put up in that primitive, fang-and-claw struggle.

Presently, as we watched, a couple of the wolves on the linger of wintertime snow jumped to their feet, facing the *couloir* and snarling. It meant that the grizzly was moving around in the gully and would come trundling out in a minute or so and go for the cubs again.

Just what was going on in Joe's mind about the wolves, cubs and bear was a puzzle to me. Off and on I'd known Joe and his uncle, Chris Walking Wolf, for more than fifteen years. With an energetic, mission-schooled wife and three small children, Joe was one of those Indians who are fighting to break free of the drab reservation life, with its stifling doles and old tribal ways, and sometimes that fight can be desperately long and hard. But in spite of my knowing him well, Joe had some dark corners in his mind, and this business of the wolves and bears was one of them.

I knew very well that his sympathies, like mine, were with the wolves. But when I threw a cartridge into the chamber of my hard-hitting Savage and remarked that I was going to take a hand when the bear came out of the *couloir*, Joe shook his head and bade me, somewhat briefly, not to interfere. The fight was his show, he'd found it and summoned me, so I stood my rifle back against a rock and let things work out however they were going to.

It was plain that Joe gave the wolves more chance of winning than I did. Also, he had the Indian's old prejudice against interfering in a fight, a prejudice inherited from the days when a band would watch with stony silence one of those wicked knife fights between two of their young bucks. But Joe had come up there to get those cubs himself, for the bounty. He'd known the dens were there and he needed the bounty money, but now he didn't seem to want to go through with the business. What had got into him I didn't know.

As we watched and waited, a large tawny wolf appeared on a hogback up the mountain and presently headed down through a boulder field toward the butte. I imagined it was just a member of the colony, returning from a hunt. But Joe studied it a minute or two and said no, it didn't belong to the pack over yonder. It was a stranger. Look at the cautious, roundabout way it was approaching the other wolves.

He proved to be right—as was usually the case when Joe and I had differences of opinion. The newcomer drew near the patch of snow hesitantly and stopped a couple of rods off. A very large male, perhaps a hundred-and-twenty-pounder, he had exceptionally rufous ears, like a Quebec timber wolf, and to myself I nicknamed him "Red-Ears."

Two of the colony wolves trotted out to meet him. Though he was rangier and heavier than either of them, Red-Ears crouched down on the ground, then turned over on his back and put his feet up in the air, asking quarter. This, Joe said, is invariably the way of the lone, wandering wolf when it comes hat in hand to a wolf colony and wants to be accepted. I had seen it twice myself, over in the tundra country at the east end of Great Slave.

The pair of wolves smelled the newcomer all over, bared their fangs at him, even gave him a nip or two. But Red-Ears lay still, and after a tense minute or so the other wolves started to wag their tails, in short, jerky fashion. Evidently this tail talk, while not entirely friendly or cordial, said that they would let him hang around, at least on a probationary basis. Thereupon Red-Ears got to his feet and stood between them stiff-legged, wagging his own tail broadly and letting himself get thoroughly inspected.

But just when I thought that Red-Ears was "in," another of the wolves on the snow patch, a medium-sized, dark-gray animal having the unusual feature of blackish legs like a fox, came rushing out all hackled up and fell upon Red-Ears viciously, slashing and biting him and trying, in the shoulder-butting way of a fighting wolf, to knock the stranger down and get at his throat.

Although Red-Ears could have whipped the black-leg individual in short order, he made no move to defend himself. Undoubtedly he knew that if he fought back he would immediately have all the other wolves on him, according to the code of the pack. For half a minute he stood his ground and took the punishment. But the other wolf kept up the one-sided fight, and presently Red-Ears broke away and ran back through the boulders, with a torn ear and a bleeding slash on his rump.

Right on the heels of this incident the bear came lumbering out of the *couloir*. He was a big, rusty-brown specimen, with a wash of dark on his face and down his backbone. While not huge, as northern grizzlies go, still he would have scaled better than nine hundred pounds, and that is a lot of grizzly any day, especially when you add a mean disposition and the battle-sharpened cunning of an oldish bear.

Before he was half a dozen steps from the gully the wolves were up and off the snow patch and streaming in to the attack. At first the fight was only a sort of skirmish. They kept circling around the shaggy brute, cutting across his nose and feinting lunges, to discourage and turn him. To this the bear paid no attention, except to throw a few rumbling snarls at them. At a determined, swaying jog he headed out through the heather toward the dens.

But then he reached the trampled area, a short hundred feet from the burrows, and there the wolves pitched into him proper, suddenly, all of them, as though by some signal. Their assault was so savage that the grizzly stopped and reared up. On both sides of him and behind him the wolves went flashing in for a snap or bite and darting out again, while the bear kept twisting this way and that and swiping at them.

Those powerful blows, with three-inch, steel-hook claws at the end of them, seemed to be missing by a hair's-breadth only. The wolves were incredibly quick, and at this ring attack they were exceedingly skillful, evidently from much practice together; but the bear too was fast and nimble. For so massive an animal he was astonishingly agile and swivel-jointed; and you knew, as you watched, that pretty soon he was going to catch one of them with one of those deadly swipes.

And pretty soon he did. A wolf that took a slash at his flank was a split-wink slow in getting back out. The bear's claws caught it on the rump and plowed all the way up to its shoulder, tearing the wolf's hide dreadfully, and the blow itself sent the wolf crashing against a rock. Bone-broken and dying, it dragged itself off on its two front legs, and the battle went on.

The trouble was that the wolves could not vitally hurt the bear. His mat of fur was too thick, for one thing. You could see they were trying to hamstring him, as they usually do when they tackle big animals, but that heavy fur went clear to his heels, and besides he was shrewd enough to keep his hind legs well up under him. The wolf has a plenty punishing bite. They can shear off a hickory-heart ax handle with one snap of their powerful carnassial teeth, and the slash of their fangs is like the rip of a walrus skinning hook. So the pack were giving the big grizzly plenty to think about. But they could not possibly drag him down or maim him or do very much except stop him temporarily.

While the individual wolves showed different degrees of bravery and experience, they were all resolute warriors—with one exception. By now I was noticing that the black-leg male had a good-sized streak of yellow in him and was shirking his part of the battle. The other wolves,

even the two females, who were still gaunt from the suckling siege, went lunging all the way in and got in their
bite or slash, but the black-leg animal kept himself well
out of danger. His ferocious, snarling lunges were fakes.
He never once delivered a bite, never once got within
arm's length of the grizzly. It was as clear an example
as I have ever seen of the fact that animals differ very
much indeed in character and personality. Not so much,
perhaps, as humans but still a great deal.

After fighting off the wolves for a few minutes, the
bear began working over toward the edge of the butte.
Whether or not this move was just an accident, or
whether it was a calculated strategy learned from other
battles, I don't know. But as he pivoted and swiped, he
kept sidling closer and closer to the high cliff edge, till
finally he was out on the very lip of the sheer rock.

If the maneuver really was a piece of cunning, it was as
shrewd as anything the wolves showed, if not shrewder.
For now the bear had complete protection on one side,
and had only to defend himself in the one direction. The
scales already had been weighted heavily in his favor and
this added advantage made the wolf cause nearly hope-
less, as even Joe grudgingly admitted.

With a queer, sidewise crab-walk, the bear kept edging
steadily nearer the dens, not stopping now but merely
swiping at the most savage of the lunges. You could see
that the wolves were baffled and bewildered. The ring of
their attack had suddenly become only half a ring, and

they didn't know what to do about that. Their lunges had to be straight in and straight back out, instead of a glancing slash. They got into one another's way, and that was damaging to their tactics as a pack and dangerous to them as individuals. And they seemed fully aware that any slight miscalculation of a lunge would send them hurtling over that hundred-and-fifty-foot cliff and crashing on the sharp, jagged traprock below.

With a fight like that in front of your eyes, you didn't give much attention to other things. Like the scavenger ravens already gathering, some flapping over the butte impatiently, some perching in the dead jackpines. Or like the hoary marmots up the mountain slope, dozens of them, all sitting bolt upright and whistling excitedly. The stranger wolf, Red-Ears, had evidently drifted back to the butte some while ago and had been edging up, but I hadn't noticed him. Then, all at once, I saw him again as he rushed in and began taking part in the fight.

One of the pack had driven him away but that didn't make any difference. Here was a battle between his tribe and the bear tribe, and he pitched into it. He was an outstanding fighter, big, fierce, fresh to the struggle, and more daring than any of them, daring to the point of being foolhardy. I remember thinking that he wouldn't last very long, with those reckless, breathtaking lunges at the front quarters of the grizzly.

And still no interference out of Joe. He had reached for his own gun, and I had the impression that once the bear got to the dens Joe wouldn't just sit there and see the grizzly gobble up the cubs. But that was only what you would expect. It didn't explain the stew of indecision inside of Joe or give me any indication what he intended to do about the cubs himself.

He was really in a situation, Joe was. Owing to family sickness and his not being able to land a decent-paying job on one of the river freight-barges that open season, Joe was badly in need of money. Particularly he wanted to buy a little roll-and-spill gold-washing machine that would double or triple what he could make with his old tomrocker, on a river-sand deposit he was working. In those two wolf litters there were thirteen or fourteen cubs; the bounty on them would make the half down payment on that machine and also would bring it across from Yellowknife by air freight. So he had come back in there to get the cubs. But instead of doing that, something had got into him and he had just sat there and watched the dens. And then the grizzly had come along.

The bear by now was only a couple of rods from the dens, and consequently the wolves were getting desperate in their attempts to stop him. In those last twenty seconds before the fight was suddenly over, I saw what a "bear hug" really is like. One of the female wolves made a suicidal lunge at the bear's throat. She must have grabbed hold and hung on, because the bear pinioned her between his huge forearm and chest. The hug itself, I'm sure, broke every rib in her body. But besides that the grizzly came up with a hind foot, socked his claws into the wolf and with a down kick just about tore her in two pieces.

That, though, brought on the end of the fight and the end of the bear. Two of the wolves, Red-Ears and another male, came lunging in together and hit the grizzly at the same instant, fairly high up, around the throat and shoulders. They must have hit him when he was more or less standing on one hind leg, and hit him pretty solidly. However it was, the impact of their lunges threw him off balance. One of the wolves managed to scramble back safely, but Red-Ears and the bear went over the rock together, the wolf sort of writhing in the air, the grizzly clawing and gouging at the cliff face for a few feet before he gave up and started falling free.

Down on the talus rock they hit a couple of yards apart, and neither of them moved much after they hit.

It took Joe and me half an hour to get across the gorge and up to the bluff. Joe collected the ears of the dead wolves—and also of the cowardly black-leg individual. We saw him skulking around up the boulder slope and both of us cut down on him, and one of us got him. So Joe had a little wad of bounty money after all, though it wasn't a third of what he needed to get the gold-washing machine.

We walked on out to the dens, and the wolves, which had defended their young so savagely and valiantly against the bear, made not the slightest move to attack or even threaten us. Watching us anxiously, they sneaked around through the boulders and brush, keeping a good hundred yards away. The surviving female came in a little closer and you could see she was badly disturbed about her bairns, but she never once snarled at us; she merely watched us with anxious, fearful eyes.

At the dens Joe got out a small round mirror—I imagine he swiped it from his wife's compact, for this trip—and shined it back into the dark burrows. Such a much of wolf cubs you never laid eyes on, back in there—a wriggling, frightened, crowding bushel and a peck of legs, tails, ears, noses and wide-open, misty pup eyes.

Joe muscled back in far enough to get a cub by the hind leg, pulled it out, showed it to me, and then sat there holding it for a minute or so.

Only then, as I watched him stroke the little thing, blow on its nose and talk to it in Cree, did I realize that Joe belonged to the Wolf Totem of the Mountain Eyinews (Crees) and that killing those wolfkins would have been a sort of sacrilege with him. Down at the post he had decided to do it, under the pressure of family need, but even down there it had been a punishing battle inside of him. And when he came up the mountain, slipped into the rocks and watched the cubs playing around in the bright sun, he'd found he didn't want the money that bad. Maybe it was because small wolf cubs are cute little things. Or maybe he got to thinking, Cree-wise, about his own bairns at home, and remembering the old tribal prohibition against harming one's totem creature. And thinking, maybe, that as he did to the cubs yonder, so the Keetchee Manitou would do to his own three Wolfkins.

Saga of the Wolf—Part I

THAT vanishing American, the wolf, is the most maligned creature in our land, bar none. For more than three centuries it has been accused of crimes it never committed. Of a ferocity toward humans that is completely alien to its real nature. Of destructiveness to game herds which naturalists who have studied the subject tell us simply isn't true. And so on, through a long list of accusations and misconceptions which have no basis whatever in actuality.

Do Wolves Attack Humans?

Let us take up, here, just one of those false charges: that wolves in the wild are a peril to humans; that they will attack and kill humans if they get half a chance; that they have done so in the past repeatedly and do so today, in Alaska and Canada.

The man in the street believes this charge implicitly. With him the very word "wolf" connotes something savage, bloodthirsty, dangerous. You can't blame him for believing so. He was brought up on the Little Red Riding

Hood tradition about wolves and never was in a position to learn the facts. On the contrary, the fiction he reads, the radio he listens to, the Western motion picture and TV he sees, always depict the wolf as a vicious and cruel beast, the slavering villain of the outdoors, the menacing enemy of the lone cowboy, occasionally the devourer of the unwary trapper or wilderness traveler.

Now, is this picture true? Or even partly true? Those who, like myself, have had some personal experience with wolves and also have made a study of the animal, know the clear answer to that question. The government field scientists know. The trappers, mounted policemen and prospectors of the North, who have a grass-roots familiarity with the animal, will every one tell you the same story, that the wolf is entirely harmless to man. The cold-sober, documented truth is simply this:

The wolf never attacks a human. Singly or in packs, hungry or not hungry, in the North, West or anywhere else, the wolf never attacks a human. And it never did. In three centuries of American and Canadian history there is not one authentic instance of wolves attacking and killing a human. Not one instance.

This statement, I know, will flabbergast many people. But regardless of that, regardless of all the vivid tales to the contrary, my statement is the strict, literal truth. For more than forty years now every reported or rumored attack by wolves on humans in the United States and Alaska has been investigated by the Fish and Wildlife authorities, and in every case they have said that the report was unfounded. Newspapers in wolf country, where stories about wolf attacks get laughed out of court, have carried standing offers of rewards for an authenticated instance of an attack, and never have they had to pay off. I personally have offered similar rewards, half a dozen times, in newspapers and magazines, and never had to pay off.

In the yearly summary of vital statistics, here and in Canada, you will find figures on people who died of snake bite, spider bite, even bee stings, or on people who got killed by cross bulls, feral dogs and other animals; but you can look back as far as the records go and you will not find one death listed as due to a wolf or a wolf pack.

So much, right now, for the hoary old myth about wolves being dangerous to humans. Later on I'll come back to this myth and explain how it grew up, and also explain a certain deep trait in wolf nature which makes it unthinkable that the animal would attack a man.

The Twilight of the Tawny Packs

Today the wolf stands in the creeping shadows of extinction. In most of our states and in all the areas best fitted for its survival it has already been exterminated. In a few scattered pockets, mostly back in barren, inhospitable regions, it still holds out, but in very small numbers. In the United States and in all of Canada except the Northwest Territories, the wolf population has dwindled to that point which scientists who have studied the total disappearance of bird and animal species call "critical"—a level below which a species suddenly becomes extinct.

Considering the long and relentless battle against wolves and considering that certain powerful groups right today are demanding their complete extermination, the astonishing thing is that we have any wolves left at all. The fact that a few survive is a tribute to the animal's braininess and its ability to exist in the rugged, bleak regions into which the remnants of the species have been driven. But all its braininess and survival power can't save it from thoughtless, uninformed persecution and from the super-deadly weapons developed against it and the coyote in the last ten years or so.

The small southern wolf, *Canis niger*, has been completely exterminated east of the Mississippi River. In all its former eastern range, extending from the Ohio Valley and southern Virginia down through the southern and Gulf states, not one single animal remains. West of the Mississippi this wolf exists here and there in small groups, sometimes only one last pair of the animals. Its total number in that great region comprising southern Missouri, Arkansas, Oklahoma, Texas and Louisiana is estimated to be under a thousand. This is a critically low and thin-spread population. A few of the larger groups may be holding their own as to numbers but the smaller groups are disappearing one by one.

The common wolf, *Canis lupus*, the big gray boy, is

holding out in mountain fastnesses in the West and a few spots elsewhere. Our largest remnant of them is in the region comprising Upper Michigan, northern Wisconsin and Minnesota. Significantly this same range contains the largest and most vigorous deer herd in America. The biology experts like to point out this fact as an answer to the charge that "wolves and big game don't mix."

It was only a few decades ago that the buffalo stood on the verge of extinction. You and I and every other Canadian and American are glad now that this magnificent animal, so symbolic of our West, was saved in the nick of time and built back up till there is no longer any danger that the species may be lost. All that this took was a little genuine information about the buffalo, a program for its conservation, and, above all, some interest in it on the part of the general public.

These same factors can, at this late date, save the wolf. But they must start operating now, without delay. For the wolf, as a species, is in grave danger, worse than the buffalo ever faced. It is far lower in numbers, except in northern Canada, and it is much more the victim of misinformation, prejudice, even hatred. In the last analysis, what happens to the wolf from here on out is up to you and me. The federal authorities, both in the United States and in Canada, will have to go on and exterminate the wolf if public opinion so directs them, whether they wish to or not.

So I want to tell you, in these pages, a few of my own

personal experiences with wolves—and rather lively those incidents were!—and also tell you the three-hundred-year saga of the wolf in America. Then I want to give you the summary judgments of authorities about *Canis lupus*. And lastly I will try to explain the basic nature of the wolf—an insight which took me many years to gain and which flatly contradicts many of the popular notions about this odd, friendly, enigmatic creature.

My purpose I will state briefly and openly: I want you to form your own opinion about the wolf, on the basis of the incontrovertible facts, good and bad, and then decide for yourself whether or not it deserves the extermination threatening it.

The Time I Was "Attacked" by Wolves

Formerly, whenever I heard or read one of those stories about some person getting attacked by a ferocious wolf pack and escaping by the skin of his teeth, I would tell myself that this person either was deliberately untruthful or else had a free-wheeling imagination. But then, one time, I learned that this wasn't necessarily so.

It happened one murky November day, in the wild hill region between the Gatineau and the Lieve (in the upper Laurentian country), when I unexpectedly found myself practically looking down the gullets of seven full-grown timber wolves.

Geologist Vlad and I had gone up there from Montreal on a bush-cruising trip but on that last afternoon of our stay we were shooting a few grouse to take home. A couple of hundred yards apart, we were going down rocky, converging draws or ravines. When one of us flushed a grouse he'd give a whistle, and if the bird flipped across the ridge the other person would get a good shot.

An excited shout from Vlad had me all set for several grouse to come arching over the ridge. But instead of grouse it gave wolves. Down the draw seven large tawnies suddenly poured around a bend a hundred and fifty feet away and came galloping straight towards your bug-eyed reporter.

Now, I realized that those wolves had been flushed and were just trying to get gone, and rationally I knew I was in no danger from them. In the Great Slave and Mackenzie regions, where the animal is not yet a rarity, I had had some personal familiarity with *Canis lupus*, and over a big spread of the Territories I had made a point of gathering field information about wolves from trappers, mounted policemen and others, and in all that huge country I had never heard of a wolf attacking or even molesting a human.

But this rational knowledge sort of came unstuck as those seven big, cinnamon-eared tawnies kept coming my way full tilt. They got bigger and more of them every jump. Finally I remembered I had a shotgun, and more or less defensively I began shooting. The gun was a 7-shot, 12-gauge pump, with Number 4 shot. That load at that distance—less than a hundred feet by then—will kill any wolf dead. In that narrow ravine a cool hunter might have bowled over every last one of the pack. Any sort of shooting would have got three or four. I didn't knock down a wolf. Or even pink one. Altogether it was one of the fanciest cases of buck fever on record.

When they were no more than forty feet from me the wolves separated, several to each side, and curved around me up against the steep ravine walls, like bobsleds on a banked turn. On above they flowed together again and disappeared in the rocks and brush.

When Vlad came across, he followed the tracks a few rods, looked for blood splotches, found none, and got the idea that I had missed those wolves deliberately. I allowed him to think so. He knew wolves and was fond of them, and I was ashamed to admit that for a few moments I had thought that a pack of them really had jumped me.

The more I reflected about this incident, the more I realized that if it had happened to somebody who was full of the usual misinformation about wolves and lacked any actual acquaintance with them, he might in all good faith have sworn that the brutes had rushed him and had been scared off in the last split-wink by the flash and bang of his gun.

Many, many encounters with wolves—when they follow you, or belly up close to your campfire, or get excited by freshly killed game or flensed carcasses—can easily be misinterpreted as an attack or threat of attack.

However, it must be said that a lot of the stories, perhaps the majority of them, about battles with wolf packs are deliberate untruths. And the savage, man-eating animal of film and fiction shows that the author is naïvely ignorant about his subject or else simply doesn't care a hang about telling the truth. It reminds me of those wondrous wild steers that crop up occasionally in cowboy fiction—steers so wild and in country so remote that they have never glimpsed a human!

The winter following my encounter with the seven wolves was very severe all across Canada. From Quebec to the Rockies the exceptional cold and the heavy snows brought wolves drifting down into districts that ordinarily were wolf-free. Most of the newspaper stories about these displaced packs were honest, factual accounts, but a few were lurid yarns about hairbreadth escapes, settlers besieged in their cabins, people perched in trees all night, and even variations of that old droshky-on-the-dead-run story, from eastern Europe.

The only comment necessary about all those yarns is that a five hundred dollar reward for any proved instance of a wolf attacking a human was given wide publicity that winter, and the reward went uncollected.

Many stories about "roving wolf packs" give the idea that wolves are homeless, wandering animals, marauding here and there promiscuously. The fact is that wolves have homes and like to stay put. It's true that prolonged bad weather and a failure of the food supply may cause them to drift considerable distances once in a while, and

wolves that follow migrant herds, like buffalo and caribou, naturally can't have any settled abode. But ordinarily the wolf has a home range and is very fond of it. In
the western states a typical wolf range would be a circuit
fifty to a hundred miles around. It would have weather
shelters like caves, a few water holes, scores of scent stations, favorite places to hunt rabbits and larger game, a
home den during the whelping season, food caches sometimes, dust wallows to keep down fleas and ticks, lookout
points, and lay-up fastnesses.

Though they can cover a lot of ground in a hurry if
they have to, a wolf or wolf family spends five to ten
days making the round of their home circuit. They travel
it counter-clockwise—why, nobody knows—and they
keep to sand or soft dirt as much as possible to spare their
feet. In the North, also, wolves have a home range, except
for the "caribou wolves," but instead of hunting around a
circuit they tend to fan out daily from some central place,
like a cave or overhang or thick-timber shelter.

DIGGING OUT A WOLF DEN

That harsh winter, dislodging and scattering wolves,
was responsible for an astonishing and instructive little
episode that happened in late May the next spring. I'd
gone out to a resort town twenty miles north of Montreal
and holed up in the lodge of a friend to finish off a book.
One afternoon a nursemaid of the neighborhood came
rushing back from a pram stroll and reported that she had

seen a big, vicious-looking dog lurking in a woods at the dead end of our street. I pocketed a gun and went down there. Several nursemaids and young mothers of that vicinity were in the habit of taking their toddlers down to that commons, and some half-wild dogs had recently attacked a man close by.

Except for a shady picnic clearing at the near side, the twelve-acre commons was thick-grown and almost impenetrable. Soon after I got there I spotted a big, dark-gray animal watching me from back in the brush. Though I couldn't see it well, it looked mighty like a wolf, and when it presently disappeared, its quiet fadeaway suggested a wolf more than a dog.

I got back into the woods by wading along a small, shallow stream that wound through it. The gravel bars and mud banks were covered with big tracks, but I couldn't tell if these were dog or wolf. There is no sure way to distinguish. Typically the wolf track is longish, the dog's roundish, and the two front toenails of the wolf show up plainer. But the difference is so slight that even the expert is often stumped.

The animal was paralleling me out in the brush, and pretty soon I got a good look at it. That, I thought, was no dog. It carried its tail horizontally like a wolf, and it had rufous ears and a wash of black on its back, and plainly it was afraid of me. That timidity was the real tip-off. Timidity towards humans is the mark of the wolf every time. Once I asked a trapper at Fort Providence, where the big, tawny sled-dogs were dead ringers for wolves, if he could always tell the difference between a wolf and a dog.

"Sure," he said. "Easy. Go aim a kick at the critter, and if it takes your laig off it's a dawg, but if it ups and runs away it's a wollif."

This remark may sound purely humorous but it does set off the essential difference between the big northern dog and the wolf. People in the North are never afraid of wolves but they are always cautious about the big huskies, and several pretty dreadful incidents are on record where dogs have killed people. At many of the posts the Mounted have a standing order to shoot any loose dog on sight.

It was amazing to find a wolf there almost within hailing distance of a big city like Montreal. But a couple of them had been shot that winter in the lower Laurentians, and evidently here was another bit of blizzard-drifted jetsam from the Haut Quebec bush. The fact that it was living at the edge of a town when there were unsettled, wooded hills within a few miles wasn't particularly surprising. In wolf country it's fairly common for individuals to hang around cabins, posts, towns. These are called "slinkers." You hear it said that slinkers are always old wolves or "gummers"—their teeth worn down or lost— and that they hang around for food. This just isn't true, and it's an important point. Wolves in the prime of life and with game easily available will live close to man if they're not shot at or otherwise driven away.

By this time I was ready for anything that might happen, and it happened—I edged around a curve in the stream and came bang onto a den and a litter of wolf cubs.

Located near the top of the stream bank, the big burrow led back under a mat of roots, and a large apron of excavated dirt sloped down to the gravel bar. The majority of wolf dens are shallow affairs, merely a few feet of entrance tunnel and a lay-up chamber; but the big apron of dirt at this one told me that the female wolf had tunneled 'way back in, probably because of the nearness to humans and dogs.

Only two cubs were outside but I felt sure there were others in the den. The ground for yards all around was littered with evidence of the she-wolf's nightly foraging —remains of chickens, ducks, cottontails, woodchucks and other food things. When I walked on up, after a few minutes, and examined this den refuse carefully, I found that the wolf had been raiding somebody's warren of Checkered-Giant rabbits. Also, I could have told some people what had happened to their missing cats.

The two fuzzy, impish cubs, about seven weeks old, were mighty cute little rascals, big feet and all. The markings on one suggested that the wolf had mated with a large dog, as they readily will. Trappers in the Territories frequently stake out their female sled-dogs, claiming that the resultant half-wolf strain is hardier and more tractable than the straight husky. The mounted police experimented with this at Fort Smith, and their hybrids were certainly far safer and more manageable than the pure huskies of the adjoining kennels. The majority of the so-called "badman wolves" of the West were female wolves, and they added insult to injury by luring away ranch dogs and mating with them.

Something had to be done about this wolf den, I decided, before one of those neighborhood scares developed. The best procedure, it seemed to me, was to dig out the den and then dispose, somehow, of the cubs and female.

Back at the lodge, I phoned in to Montreal to a couple of the fellows in our skeet and fishing gang. They got all steamed up about digging out a wolf den and said they'd collect several of the other fellows and be out right after work.

As luck would have it, I was summoned home to Montreal by an unexpected business matter and didn't get to go along that evening. I wasn't needed; five of the gang showed up, including Vlad, armed with shovels, mattocks and refreshments. According to their reports afterward, digging out that den was a backbreaking job—a long deep tunnel through roots, rocks and hardpan. They dug from six o'clock till dark at ten-thirty. Then they built a fire and dug till long after midnight.

Most of the time, they said, the female wolf lay in the

brush just across the stream and watched them. Never once did she growl or show any threat.

When they got the den dug out, an argument developed about how to dispose of the wolf family. At first the majority opinion, Vlad dissenting, was to do away with the cubs and shoot the female. But gradually this opinion changed. Though the fellows didn't say so, I believe that the silent, patient she-wolf, lying at the edge of the firelight and begging them with her eyes not to harm her bairns, was the thing that softened them up. At any rate, it ended with Vlad having his way. When they finally reached the six cubs and tumbled them into a sack, Vlad and another fellow took up the sack, made sure the wolf knew her cubs were in it, and then started out on foot for a hill spur five miles west, with the wolf following along behind them.

If there's one thing above everything else that animals will fight for, it's their young. I've often wondered, thinking about this incident, if there is one other animal on earth, a good-sized animal like a wolf, that would have lain there in the brush and suffered those men to dig out her den and sack up her cubs without so much as a snarl. No, I just don't believe there is.

WEREWOLVES

Undoubtedly, one of the main contributing factors in people's unreasoning hostility toward wolves is that ancient, Old Country business known as lycanthropy. This means the myths, superstitions and other folklore concerning werewolves; about humans turning into wolves and vice versa, about witches and wizards who assume wolf shape for their sinister doings, about wolves raising children, and so on.

Modern research has led anthropologists to believe that our fear of wolves, along with the more archaic myths about them, goes back to a vastly remote age. In the most ancient Eurasian languages the word for wolf was "leo-pes," from which "lupus" is derived. Now, "leo-pes" means lion-footed, and this term isn't descriptive of the true wolf at all but of a different animal, the so-called dire wolf or cave wolf, a large carnivore now extinct. Hence anthropologists believe that the original wolf-lore or lycanthropy referred to the dire wolf. If this is so, then those original fears and myths were well-founded indeed; those tremendous Pleistocene "wolves" must have made life miserable for the humans of that time. Incidentally, our modern wolves and dogs (*Canis*) are not descendants of the dire wolf but are only distant, collateral relatives.

However all that may be, the fact remains that lycanthropy is very old, deep-rooted and widespread in the Old World. Lycanthropy is one of the most ancient of human beliefs; at the dawn of history it was already hoary with age. There is "black lycanthropy," which is evil, and "white lycanthropy," which is beneficent. The Romulus and Remus legend is an example of beneficent relationship.

The berserk superstitions of the Baltic, the *loup-garou* myths of middle Europe, and the famous "vampire were-wolves" of the Ukraine are examples of black lycanthropy.

It's a temptation to consider these myths and legends as so much nonsense and toss them out the window. To be sure, the supernatural part of lycanthropy is contrary to reason, but this folklore does have a few aspects of practical importance. Take the word "lycanthrope." This means a person who believes that a wolf's spirit has taken possession of him. He goes on all fours like a wolf, eats, drinks and howls like one, bites his family and friends and tries to flee to the woods. This affliction is not a superstition but a medically recognized form of insanity, rather rare over here but not uncommon in the Old Lands.

Or take the widespread folk belief that the blacksmith had power to exorcise "wolf madness" (hydrophobia) out of a person. That certainly sounds like superstition, pure and silly. But it had a core of solid, practical value. Before Pasteur's time rabies was possibly the most dreaded of all afflictions. A person bitten by a rabid dog, wolf or human was hauled before the blacksmith and given the "treatment." Of course, the mumbo-jumbo part of this procedure was valueless, but the smith's red-hot cauterizing iron very often kept the dread malady from developing.

In its purely superstitious aspects, lycanthropy never took much root in the New World. It had, and still has, some foothold among the French Canadians, and it bobbed up a time or two as a minor note in the witchcraft hubbub. But otherwise America has never been troubled by werewolves.

However, just about all the rest of the age-old European hostility against the wolf did come across the water as invisible baggage of the early Colonials. The nursery rhymes and tales, with their emotional overtones; the belief that wolves attack and kill humans; the ascription of all sorts of villainous traits to the wolf—this we did inherit from Europe. It set the mold and form of common opinion, and largely that opinion has remained unchanged to this day. It's unfactual, it's unenlightened, it's flatly contrary to the scientific truth, and it's a cruel injustice to one of the finest creatures of the outdoors, and I think it's high time that we rid our minds of it.

Saga of the Wolf—Part II

THE story of the buffalo, the passenger pigeon and others of our native fauna have been told and retold, but the story of the wolf in America, a tale much more dramatic and economically important, has gone almost unknown. This three-hundred-year battle between man and wolf in the New World was another contributing factor in the bad reputation of the wolf, and in this instance we must admit that the animal did in large measure deserve his bad name.

IN COLONIAL TIMES

For a full hundred years after the first settlers came over, "ye devouring wulff" was easily the most hated creature in the land. And for good reason. It caused more damage than the bear, puma, bobcat and all other "Wilde Vermin" put together. This Eastern wolf, *Canis lupus lycaon*, existed in great numbers. Issuing from its safe retreat in the virgin woods, the "ravening runnagadoes" coursed the farmlands by night and destroyed the settlers' cows, horses, pigs, sheep and poultry.

In those days people had very poor weapons and defenses against "ye noxious wulves." Woven-wire fencing, which is the only practical wolf guard, was nonexistent. Metal traps were not yet being manufactured, except for a few clumsy, handwrought things. The crude firearms were not much employed in wolf hunting, and strychnine or "wolf bane" didn't come into use in this country till long later.

The most successful device the early colonists had, and it was only moderately effective, was the wolf pit or "wulfe penne." These took considerable labor to build, and many were in continuous use for several generations. A few are still extant, though badly caved in. One that I examined and measured, in the Sherbrooke country, was typical of the larger and more elaborate pits. It was a circular trench eight feet deep (estimate) and twenty feet across, with walls of rough masonry. The trench was about six feet wide. This left a vertical column eight feet in diameter in the middle of the pit. On top of this column, which the farmer reached by a plank or footlog, was tethered a live pig, sheep, goose, or offal from butchering. When the "greedie wulfes" tried to get at the bait, they broke through the screen of small branches and grass which covered the trench, and fell down into the pit.

To dispose of the "hiddeous howlers" in the "penne," did the settler waste precious powder and ball by shooting them? He did not. He simply climbed down into the trench and "dispatched the wolfes with a bludgeon."

That's right—with an ax or club; that was the usual way. Speaking of a much later time, in the Ohio Valley, Audubon tells how he watched a farmer climb down into a pit containing six wolves, hamstring the animals one by one and heave them out for his dogs to finish off.

Jumping into a pit among six wolves, without even an ax or club but only a knife—that certainly doesn't sound as though the people of those days considered the wolf any ferocious man-eater.

Some of the early chronicles do state in a general way that "ye nighte dogges" were dangerous to man, but they cite no specific instances of attacks on humans. Furthermore, these same chronicles, a few paragraphs farther on, will flatly contradict themselves by calling the wolf a "fearsome curr" or a "greate coward." Several of those early chroniclers even state outright that they have never known of a wolf setting upon a man or a woman. Undoubtedly those vague statements about the wolf being dangerous were merely reflections of the evil reputation of the wolf in Europe.

It is significant that the Pilgrims started paying bounty on the "wullve" just a few years (1630) after the landing at Plymouth. Evidently the wolf was a real economic problem. The bounty, about half a pound per wolf, was a costly business for those impoverished people. In Virginia the bounty system was started in 1632, and later the practice was adopted nearly everywhere, along with other control measures. Some communities hired their local

Daniel Boone on a year-round basis to range the adjacent forest and especially "too seek out ye dennes & distroye ye wolve whelppes." Indians were paid the fur value for wolf pelts and then given an extra reward in "corne & wine." Ring hunts and line drives were carried out periodically, with some success, but the wolf dogs that were imported from Europe promptly got eaten up.

At times when wolves were extra numerous and destructive, some extreme measures were resorted to. For instance, a hundred years after the Pilgrim landing a project was set up to guard Cape Cod from wolves by building a solid board fence six feet high clear across the Peninsula in the vicinity of Barnstable.

All these measures did no more than mitigate the wolf scourge a little. The abatement and final solution of the problem came about slowly and indirectly, as a by-product of the clearing of the forest and the gradual creep of population westward. When a community had a wide buffer belt of little frontier settlements and homesteads between it and the forest primeval, it was at last safe from wolf depredation and could sleep nights without having to keep the shoats under the bed and the milch cow in the summer kitchen.

One wolf incident of later colonial days (about 1740) became an Americana classic. That was, of course, the story of how Israel Putnam crawled back into the cave-den of a local badman she-wolf and shot it. One hundred years of American school youngsters read this piece of derring-do in their McGuffey and Baldwin readers, and this original story was the inspiration of scores of newspaper stories later on, here and there. The school-text account, while lively and graphic enough, is tame and pale compared with those newspaper and early magazine versions. The wolf was a "monster," a "demon of the desert," a "fell and bloody beast." Her eyes were balls of baleful fire, her fiendish growls issuing from the cave froze the blood of the group waiting outside, and the way she "rattled" her teeth scared even the doughty Israel back out twice before he finally completed his job.

That Putnam Wolf story became traditional in American journalism—the traditional and standard way to handle a wolf account. Incredible or not, some of those lurid phrases still linger in modern press treatments of any piece of wolf news that gets onto the wires.

We suspect that the unknown genius who penned that first account of Putnam and the wolf did so with tongue in cheek. In the first place our twenty-second cousin, old don't-shoot-till-you-see-the-whites-of-their-eyes Putnam, never in his life had to take three hitches before facing wolves, redcoats or any other peril. In the second place, there was nothing heroic whatever in crawling back into a wolf den, and that original reporter couldn't have helped knowing this. In those days, and for decades afterward on the advancing American frontier, little boys in the springtime went along wolf hunting with their daddies for the express purpose of crawling into wolf dens. That is, boys of seven or eight who were skinny enough to get into a wolf hole, would crawl back into the den and drag out the cubs for the bounty.

This, also, certainly doesn't sound as though the wolf was regarded as any savage, dangerous animal.

ONLY TWO SPECIES OF WOLF

While the early settlers from Carolina southward had considerable trouble with wolves, they had no such woe as the settlers we've been talking about, in the middle and northern colonies. This was because the southern settlers were dealing with a different wolf, *Canis niger*.

We may as well tackle right here that endless argument about the many allegedly different species of wolves in our land. Scientists have studied literally thousands of specimens, present-day and all the way back to wolf skeletons from ancient Indian mounds, and in spite of the wide variations in color, size and habits, the modern tendency is to recognize just two species of wolves in North America: *Canis niger* and *Canis lupus*.

For whatever my opinion is worth, I myself am not entirely satisfied with this classification, unless we regard the Eastern wolf (*lycaon*) as the result of a massive cross-breeding between *C. lupus* and *C. niger*. But in all important respects this two-species classification is soundly based on facts and is agreed with by the best modern authorities.

The Gray Wolf

First, let us discuss *Canis lupus*. That's the big boy, the common wolf, the animal we've dealt with so far. In different regions he is called the Eastern wolf, the lobo, the buffalo wolf, the gray, timber, Barren Grounds and Arctic wolf, but all these variations are the same species. Like most creatures, he is smallest in his southern range, largest in the northern. *C. lupus* varies in weight from seventy pounds for the Sonoran lobo to one hundred fifty pounds or even more for the huge wolf of northern Keewatin and the lower Mackenzie.

The predominant hue of this wolf is gray or tawny, but he may be black, white, reddish or any combination of these. Incidentally, the big, creamy-white, silky-furred wolf of the far North is a strikingly beautiful creature. The tremendous white pelts which you occasionally see at the Edmonton or Montreal fur auctions may awe you but they give little conception of what the living wolf is like, drifting through an evergreen thicket or loping across a granite swell in the Thelon of the Barren Grounds.

The wolf of Europe is the identical same animal as our *Canis lupus*. This arouses the question: "Does the European wolf attack humans? Surely those innumerable stories to this effect can't all be wrong—or can they?"

That's a question I'll have to duck. No authoritative study of this has ever been made over there, at least that I know about. But I will say that I'm very dubious about those tales. It's notorious that in Europe the wolf has frequently been used as a crime cover-up; that is, a person will commit a murder or a livestock theft and fix things to make it look like wolf work. Also, Europe has always been plagued by wolflike feral dogs, which are truly vicious and dangerous. In the last generation the Ukraine and the Balkans have reported that these wild dogs, and also the genuine wolf, are very much on the increase. This

is probably due to the fact that the possession of guns and ammunition by farmers, herders and woodsmen is a serious "crime" in the Iron Curtain countries.

Here is one example of the untrustworthiness of those European stories. Last year my press-clipping service on wolves came up with an account, widely reprinted in this country, about wolves attacking numerous people in a certain small country over there. I found out the name of the correspondent who wrote that account and dropped him a letter asking if he was sure that his source of information was reliable. In a few weeks I had his reply. He stated that he personally looked into this matter after my letter and ascertained that roving animals in this province in question really had attacked people and killed considerable livestock, but that these animals were not genuine wolves but wild dogs. The reason that people reported this as wolf work was that because of some provincial law they received recompense for wolf depredation but not for damage that dogs did.

THE SOUTHERN WOLF

Our other species of wolf is *Canis niger,* and it is found only in the New World. Common names for it are: southern wolf, red wolf, swamp wolf, Ozark, Delta, Oklahoma, Florida, etc. From its Latin name you would think that this wolf is black. Well, a few of them are—an intense, shiny black. But much oftener this species is reddish, with bright-rusty ears, nose and legs, and blackish king hairs down its backbone and out to the end of its tail. But it can be almost any color (except white).

This southern wolf is quite small. Adults weigh from thirty-five pounds to a maximum of sixty-five. This is coyote size, and the two animals are sometimes confused. In southern Missouri I once argued half a night with a storeful of fellows about an animal which somebody had shot and brought in. They swore it was a wolf, but you could tell at a glance that it was nothing but a coyote. Its muzzle was sharp, its ears narrow and pointed, its face and **ex-**pression foxlike, its nose pad (rhinarium) much too narrow for any wolf.

Although the coyote is sometimes called a brush wolf, prairie wolf, swamp wolf, it is no wolf at all. In its anatomy, habits and nature it is a different creature.

Because of its small size the southern wolf seldom attacks horses or cattle, or medium-sized livestock like pigs. In fact, its habits are such that it usually is not much of a menace even to small livestock or poultry. I do not mean that it never raids a farmstead. Definitely it will. But compared with its bold and swashbuckling big brother, it is a skulker, tending to avoid farms and the vicinity of man, and keeping to the fastnesses of swamps and lonely hills. Its food supply, consisting of woodchucks, mice, turtles, snakes, frogs, cotton rats, fish and suchlike, is fairly constant the year around, without the famine periods of the Great Plains or the North, and so it is not hunger-driven to depredation.

A rather silent creature, compared with the noisy coyote and the loudmouthed gray wolf, *niger* is wary, smart and an efficient hunter. It can live on little and apparently it doesn't go on "meat drunks" or indulge in unnecessary killing, as *lupus* will do with livestock when it gets a chance. But in spite of its wariness and its comparative harmlessness, *niger* is next door to being extinct. Another generation will see it entirely wiped out.

The Wolf Hunters

As the frontier pushed westward after the Revolutionary War, the battle between man and wolf rolled west with it. Our first good scientists were on the job by then, and they reported that Ohio, Indiana, Illinois and "the Dark and Bloody Ground" were overrun with wolves, preying on the abundant game herds. But the settler in the Midwest had an easier time killing them out. He had better traps and guns, and the country was not quite so hilly and rugged.

When the story crossed the Mississippi and moved out onto the Great Plains, it became the story of the buffalo, strychnine and the plains wolf. Variously called the lobo, gypsy, shepherd, loafer and buffalo wolf, this animal flourished in great numbers, preying chiefly on the shaggy herds. With rifles and traps the early hunters took a heavy toll of the plains wolf; thousands of pelts moved through St. Louis every year. But there was little diminution of the wolf numbers till strychnine came into wide use, about 1840–50.

This poison had been known for centuries and had actually been used at times by the early colonists, who gave it the name of "wolf bane." But it was unrefined, uncertain in potency, controlled by Europe, meager in supply and sky-high in price. America finally broke the monopoly by importing the nux vomica bean directly and making standardized, high-potency strychnine, and quickly this came into wholesale use against the wolf.

Typically, a "wolfer" using strychnine would get up leisurely in the morning, ride out and shoot three or four buffalo a few miles apart, skin them for the robes, salt the carcasses with "bane," and be back home eating roast buffalo hump by noon. When he rode out again the next morning he would find from one to a dozen dead wolves at each plant. He had only to flense these and ride home again. Compare this with the gruelling, dawn-to-dusk labor of the trapline. And the cost? Less than three cents per wolf. Although the beaver trapper esteemed himself the aristocrat of the fur hunters, the wolfer could buy and sell him. Wolf peltry was in big demand those days to make laprobes for the carriage trade and overcoats for the Czar's army. The wolfer got about $1.50 per pelt. The New York price was about $3.50.

The Wolf and the Ranches

While the plains wolf still existed in what one observer called "countless packs and congregations," cattle ranching was obviously impossible. Even when traps, guns and strychnine, along with the passing of the buffalo, had reduced the plains wolf to a mere fraction of its former numbers, the ranches suffered heavy losses from wolf depredation and had to wage perpetual war on the animal. Instances were common where one pack of wolves destroyed several thousand dollars worth of stock in a single night.

There can be no dispute about it—the wolf just cannot be allowed anywhere within raiding distance of range livestock. Those of us who have a secret fondness for the wolf as an incarnation of the spirit of wild, lonely regions and who hope that this fine, bold animal can be saved from extinction—we will only do the wolf a disservice if we urge that it be allowed to remain in places where it can do damage and stir up demands for its extermination.

The plains wolf had to go from the range country, and he went, but he put up a long, bitter fight. Those wolves which learned to avoid traps, guns, and poison were naturally the craftiest and wariest of their kind, and each succeeding generation, as their numbers dwindled, got still craftier and warier. Here, plainly, is the explanation of a much-argued contradiction. Nearly every early observer of the plains wolf remarked that it was tame, dumb, easy to trap or poison or shoot at pointblank range. Yet, toward the end this animal was unbelievably shrewd and hard to take. . . . It had learned.

The Outlaw Wolves

Now we come to the swan song of the plains wolf. To those few lone, super-shrewd, phanton-elusive survivors that hung on and on, well into the present century. About a dozen of those badmen wolves were as well-known in the West as the most notorious two-legged desperadoes.

They became individuals, named, described by posters, and with prices on their heads. They were hunted by posses, by expert trappers and by federal men. Sometimes half a dozen experienced hunters would be after one wolf. Yet several of these badmen wolves eluded capture and death for years.

There was the Custer Wolf of the Black Hills, probably the most notorious of them all but by no means the craftiest or most destructive. And the picturesque, daredevil Sycan Wolf of Oregon, who was definitely tabbed with fifteen thousand dollars of depredation. And the "Widow of Apishapa," a whitish-gray wolf, only medium-sized and somewhat maimed, who lured ranch dogs off to mate with her and brought back the whelps to plague the ranch. And there were the Phantom, Big Foot, Aguila, Whitey the Bob-Tailer, who specialized in de-tailing cows, and finally the worst of them all, old "Dakota Three Toes," who destroyed *fifty thousand dollars* worth of stock and survived *fourteen years* of intensive hunting.

THE WOLF IN CANADA TODAY

With the passing of the badman wolves, the three-hundred-year battle of the wolf against man was at an end in the United States. Canada still has a little trouble with them, though. In Alberta and British Columbia, where a small amount of depredation occurs in severe winters, the problem is mixed up with the much more serious problem of coyotes, which are on the increase all up through the Northern Rockies. But wolf depredation in the provinces is fast dwindling. Against our newest weapons—the airplane, the deadly cyanide set-gun, the still deadlier 1080 —the wolf just doesn't stand a chance.

Canada's main concern is over the toll that wolves take of the huge caribou herds of the Barren Grounds, and she is proceeding vigorously against the wolf with new regulations and the efficient modern weapons. In consequence the wolf population of the Northwest Territories—Mackenzie, Yukon, Keewatin and Franklin—is shrinking rapidly.

No one who has seen the spectacular caribou *traverse* of the Barrens and also seen the big packs of wolves accompanying it will deny that the packs do kill many thousands of the tundra caribou. However, this is not proof that they harm the herd or even reduce its numbers; and this is equally true of wolf depredation on deer, elk, mountain sheep, moose or any other wild game. Careful studies made in our national forests and in Alaska and Canada indicate:

1. The wolf seldom goes on orgies of destruction against wild animals, as it frequently does against the domestic sheep and cow.

2. The wolf preys chiefly on old animals past the desirable breeding age, or on sick or weak individuals.

3. The statistical effect of wolf depredation on a game herd is to keep the herd at a vigorous level. They are not unlike a storm that combs the deadwood out of a forest.

Biologists like to point out that during colonial times in the East, when the wolf population was so high, big game was at an all-time abundance there. Likewise in the West, with the buffalo, elk, antelope. As for the Barren Ground caribou, they say: "After all, those caribou have lived with the wolf for many thousands of years and yet they seem to have done all right, to judge by the millions of them."

Wolf Habits and Traits

As previously stated, the wolf in the North doesn't make a hunting circuit, as in the West, but tends to radiate out from some central point, according to the weather and game movements. The male wolves stake out this home range; that is, they warn intruders away with their scent stations.

While a range may be occupied by just one wolf family, more frequently you find two or more families living in the close association of a little colony. When a she-wolf leaves her young to go hunting, one of the other females will take charge of the cubs—a primitive form of baby-sitting. The males do most of the food gathering, and the cubs are almost never left unguarded.

A colony may consist of parents, cubs, grandparents, uncles and even wolves of no blood kinship. When a stray wolf, which has lost its own outfit, shows up, it may or may not be accepted. The stray will lie down with its feet in the air and ask quarter, exactly like a dog. If the colony males don't "cotton" to it, they give it a biting and drive it away. I believe, though, that this seldom happens. While there is an occasional wolf individual that is surly and unsocial, the average wolf is friendlier toward and gets along with other wolves much better than dogs do. You can watch a wolf colony of a dozen males for hours and not see a sign of snarling, fighting or other ill temper.

Far more than most animals, wolves have a deep, instinctive need for association. Whereas the cat nature is solitary, the dog nature is social, and the wolf is merely a wild dog. Indeed, its harsh conditions of life seem to have sharpened and deepened its social instincts. The lone, wandering wolf is a most unhappy creature. The wolf that follows you persistently, creeps up to your campfire or comes sniffing around your cabin night after night is usually a lone wolf and a lonely one. Naturally they prefer association with their own kind, but next to that wolves will try to associate with man. You see this plainest in remote regions where the wolf has been hunted little, but you see it even in slinker wolves in country where the animal has learned that man is his enemy.

If taken as a small pup and raised in an ordinary way, a wolf is practically the same as a dog. I have seen many of these animals and have inquired about others, and the chief difference seems to be that the wolf is more tractable and somewhat more affectionate toward its owner. Tame wolves can be used in sled teams, along with dogs or other wolves. They show absolutely none of the vicious, treacherous, dangerous traits connoted by the word "wolfish." As a rule they are splendidly healthy and vital animals. Super-charged may be the right term. They are always ready for a romp or tussle, but they are big, powerful things and their play is mighty rough.

Once a trapper at Resolution, tent-bound by sickness, asked me to stop by a small islet offshore and feed his wolf, Wop, which he had "parked" out there. Wop turned out to be a big young Barrens wolf sixteen months old and about one hundred ten pounds. He was pathetically glad to have a visitor. As I came in across the shallows he let loose a string of gurgley howls and cut crazy figure-eights on the landwash, quite beside himself with joy.

The feeding went off all right, but then Wop wanted to play and I made the mistake of letting him. It was like playing with an exuberant young locomotive. In spite of my "Nix, guy, nix; take it easy, now," I was considerably the worse for wear and tear before I could get back to the boat. As I left, Wop climbed up on some drift logs and howled forlornly.

Nobody except a trapper or other person living in lonely country should ever consider having a pet wolf. It eats too much, it's a big animal and makes people uneasy, it plays too rough (unintentionally) with dogs and children, and it's too freedom-loving to endure confinement well. In Edmonton I was told that some people are bringing wolf cubs back from their Alcan trips, just as automobile vacationists have been bringing coyote pups back

East for some years. This is a thoroughly bad business, for several reasons. To cite just one, some of these animals stray off, drift into the hills, mate with dogs, and pretty soon we have a pocket, in thick-settled country, of these wild, hybrid "coydogs," "dogotes" or "wolfdogs," which have to be hunted down and killed.

THE WOLF'S BASIC NATURE

In country where the wolf has been decimated by poison, trap, gun and airplane, or by the unspeakably cruel devices used by the far-Northern Indian and by the Eskimo, the survivors are not wolves in a natural state at all. Rather they are hunted outlaws, wild, distrustful and superlatively shrewd, as we saw the plains wolf become.

For a long time it was an ambition of mine to find some region where the wolf was still in a completely natural state and see what the creature really is like. It took a while to find out the truth—there is no such region left. Nowhere on the continent.

But back in the sub-Arctic Rockies lying west of the lower Liard and upper Mackenzie, we do find a few wild, mountain-locked valleys where trappers and prospectors haven't gone very much and where you can get in only if you have a geologist friend called Vlad, who sets you up to the trip on his company's plane and gas. Back in there the native wolves do give you some idea of what the creature is like in a natural state. In that harsh cold country game is scarce and wolves are not plentiful. But when

you are lucky enough to encounter them you are reminded of the "tame, dumb and trusting" animal that the
early American observers wrote about.

Back in those mountains a wolf will frequently stand
and look at you within good gun range, or lope through
the shore willows to keep watching your boat, or crawl
up close at night and study the strange, lordly creature
who is master of fire and warmth and light.

You study him back and try to figure out what brings
him to your campfire and keeps him there. Hunger? His
eyes aren't on your pack of grub in the sapling but on
you. He's a big brute, a hundred-and-forty pounder, and
he can break a caribou's neck at one bite, but he's afraid
of you. Why? By way of experiment you reach for your
rifle and point it at him, but he doesn't move—he's never
been shot at.

His fear seems to have awe and respect and friendliness
mixed in. You get to thinking that if you were clad in
skins and had only a stone ax, he would be a mighty fine
helper on the hunt—your brains and hand skills, his great
speed, courage, power. You get the impression that in
his dumb-brute way he regards you not as just another
creature, even a puzzling, formidable creature, but as
something *sacrosanct* with him. Above all, you have the
persistent feeling that he would like to be friendly.

Vlad tosses him a hunk of bread. He inches forward,
gets it, eats it, and then lies there watching you, forty feet
away. You think about those seven wolves on the Gati-

neau that time—the poor, panicky, fleeing things, terrified at finding themselves in the vicinity of man; and you realize all over again that those wild, phantomlike wolves, which are the only kind that most people ever know, aren't typical, natural wolves at all but are hunted outlaws.

Vlad agrees with you. "A dog," he remarks, "is just a wolf that came to dinner. And a wolf is just a dog that missed the bus. From the very beginning this wolf-dog or dog-wolf had some queer, exceptional instinct for associating with us humans. That's why it was our first animal friend and why it's always been our *best* friend."

FINIS

The tawny packs, both *lupus* and *niger*, have seen their great day end and twilight close in. They are on their way to extinction, make no mistake about that. And their fate is squarely up to you and me. Make no mistake about that, either.

Only a few decades ago the federal wildlife authorities had a program which called for the complete extirpation of the wolf in the United States. This program was the result of the heavy pressure on them from certain groups, a pressure which was a continuation from earlier days and different conditions. But the authorities had to listen to it. There was no pressure from the other side. Only indifference. In obedience to the demands of the interested groups they planned and largely carried out a systematic extermination of the wolf remnants in the national forests and also supervised this work on state and private lands.

But they put up a fight for the wolf, the best fight they could, and tried persistently to alter the program they were perforce carrying out. They took pains to study wolf habits, learn the facts about the animal and present these facts to the public. I believe that the following points are a reasonably good summary of expert opinion both in the United States and Canada:

1. In wild, remote districts where there can be no danger to economic interests, like livestock, the wolf should be allowed to exist, as part of our original fauna and balance of nature.

2. The alleged danger to humans, which crops up in various forms, can be regarded as entirely nonexistent.

3. The occasional individual wolf that comes out and starts depredating should be eliminated, as it easily can be now. This is known as selective control.

4. In reasonable numbers, which are nowhere exceeded now, the wolf should be regarded as a beneficial factor in regard to game herds.

This potential program seems to me informed and practical. I believe it would win out if only public opinion would get behind it and push a little.

But Vlad, the last time I saw him—a few weeks before his fatal plane crash—was gloomy about the prospects for the wolf. We had visited a fur auction that evening and walked past hundreds of pelts of the big Northern wolf, and we were talking about their growing scarcity in the Northwest Territories, their last real stronghold. The trouble was, Vlad remarked, that people can't get rid of the age-old idea that wolves are savage and dangerous animals. You can prove to them a dozen times over, he said, that the wolf never attacks a human, but they won't listen. They want it killed out. What big teeth you've got, Grandma.

"Remember that time at Montreal," he said, "when we sacked up those wolf cubs and took them back to the hills where they'd be a little safer? Those were probably the last wolves in the southern Laurentians. Well, some day you and I will dig out a wolf den here in the sub-Arctic, here on the Liard River, and carry the cubs a little farther back into the mountains. That will be the last wolves in the Rockies—or anywhere else."

Loafer Wolf

IT was a fine Indian-summer day in the Mackenzie Rock-ies. On a hogback a little above timberline Alec and I had been sitting in a nest of boulders for nearly two hours, watching and waiting. It was getting down to the tail of the afternoon but so far Alec hadn't had a glimpse of the dangerous rogue bear he'd been given the job of hunting down and killing. Nor had we seen anything of the family of wolves which he had told me about and which had been my special reason for going along with him that day.

"Looks like this trip is going to be a bust for both of us, Alec," I remarked.

Alec shook his head. "You'll see wolves. Any time now. Hot of the day's over, flies've died down, so the car-ibou'll be drifting out of the brush. For the evening browse. That'll bring the wolves out."

"How about your bear down yonder in that brush—what d'you figure his next move will be?"

"Un't know," Alec grunted. His shrug said that brown bears were tricky and unpredictable brutes. Especially when they were "casuals," or wanderers from their home range. The big, vicious brown that Alec was after had probably come from two or three hundred miles back in the sub-Arctic Rockies. "But," Alec added, "he'll be moving out of that lay-up yonder. Pretty soon. If he winds us he might sneak off and go. Or might come for us. I think he'll come for us. He's a *hiyu* bad 'un."

I certainly hoped that things would liven up, as Alec thought, because this had to be my last day in the Mackenzie country. After getting my assignments done at Edmonton and over in British Columbia, I'd taken a quick trip down north to the Arctic, stopping at Norman, Good Hope and Aklavik, to see what was new along the Big River and chew the fat with old friends. On my way back up south the plane had put down at a camp of the Condomin outfit, north of Simpson, and there I'd run smack into Alec Muheekoon, a Squamswap whom I'd known in the Lesser Slave district. In just a few days I was due back East, to see a daughter married and begin my university lecturing, but when Alec told me about the family of big, silver-gray wolves he'd been seeing in that hill-spur across Little Athebwanni Lake, I decided to squeeze out one more day and go along with him. He could hunt his half-ton bear and I would take a look at those mountain wolves.

Even in the Big Snowies of the far North it isn't every day you can see wolves *au naturel*. Mostly you see them as peltry in a fur loft or as a sorry collection of bounty ears.

As a guide and all-around bush man, Alec had been

working for the Condomin outfit at their big camp south-
west of Resolution, where the company was exploring
a huge copper field. But then their Simpson camp developed "bear trouble" and they'd flown Alec down north

to tend to it. Along the west shore of Little Athebwanni
the Condomin had thirty-some men in the bush—two
prospecting teams and a diamond-drill crew proving up—
and this rogue bear had thrown a monkey wrench into
the works. A hulking big dishface with a vicious temper,

it had demolished two location camps and come an inch of killing a couple of men, and the fellows swore they weren't going into the bush any more till that big *siam-siam* was shot.

For several days now Alec had been tracking the bear, studying its habits and gradually closing in. He'd discovered that its favorite lay-up during the heat of the day was a little, five-acre tangle of juniper, boulders and old windfall just down the southeast slope of our hogback. It was in there now, with a flock of whiskeyjacks quarreling around at it, and Alec was watching the tangle for the brute to come trundling out.

Down toward the northwest arm of the lake several mountain caribou emerged from an aspen belt and headed up the open swale in our direction. Behind them others appeared, more and more—maybe ninety in all. In straggly files they came up the swale almost halfway to us, then spread out over a thirty-acre moraine flat and began feeding in the foxtail and dwarf heather.

"Well," I said, "the caribou are out, Alec, but any wolves in this neck of the mountains I'll eat."

I'd no more than said this when five caribou came swinging over a hogback to the north of us and after them came three wolves, chasing them full tilt, with short, excited *yeolps*. I'd heard this before and knew it meant the wolves were young animals.

Two of the caribou were cows, the other three yearlings. One of these, evidently born late, was quite small.

It couldn't have been over sixty-five or seventy pounds. Yet it kept up with the others easily enough as the little group diagonaled down the long open slope toward the herd on the moraine flat.

The way those five caribou outdistanced the wolves surprised me, even though I'd seen much the same thing many times in the tundra country over east. The caribou weren't particularly scared and weren't running all out, but they made those wolves seem a bit leadfooted. It was an illustration of the fact that in an ordinary chase a caribou—or a moose, elk, antelope, or a mountain sheep on rugged ground—can drop a wolf a mile behind.

The three wolves soon realized they hadn't a chance. A few hundred yards down the slope they broke off the chase, monkeyed around in the boulders a few minutes, tried to stalk a fat hoary marmot, then trotted back up over the ridgeline.

"That was the young 'uns," Alec grunted. He had turned his head to watch the chase. "Un't know any better yet. Mebbe the old 'uns'll show up. Let old man wolf go after a caribou, you'll see something."

As we waited, I noticed that Alec kept glancing at the low sun, with a flick of worry on his swart face, and I knew what was troubling him. If that bear didn't start stirring pretty soon, he'd have to go down there to its lay-up, beat through that tangle and roust the brute, and he didn't like the idea too much. At close quarters, in that mess of brush and rocks, he might not be able to blast it down before it got to him. But at the camp across the lake thirty-some men were sitting on their thumbs, and also Alec, who had a wife and couple of kiddies at Lesser Slave, wanted the two hundred dollar bonus he'd get for killing the bear.

I was worried too. If Alec went down there, he'd of course tell me to remain on the hogback, but nevertheless I'd have to go along with him. You couldn't just sit there and let a hunting partner walk into danger alone. And I confess that I hadn't any desire whatever to go down into that tangle and mix it with that big brown.

We got to talking again, and I said: "Alec, you've seen a lot of these mountain wolves, winter and summer, and do you very often see 'em take out after a caribou and keep after it till they run it down?"

He thought for a minute. "Frisky young 'uns'll chase game a ways sometimes. Like we just saw. But old 'uns, no. Never saw 'em chase a caribou much over half a mile."

I thought, "So Alec here, with all his years of experience up and down the northern Rockies, never saw one of those chases you read so much about. Those chases that last for hours, even days." I'd never seen one myself, and all the trappers and wolf hunters I'd talked with had said likewise.

Across on the other hogback a large, silver-gray animal came into sight on the ridgeline. It was so large that I thought at first it was a caribou, a yearling, but when I put the binoculars on it I saw it was a wolf—a big, rangy, hundred-and-thirty-pound gray, with somewhat rusty ears and a wash of black down its backbone. It surely made a picture, standing over there on the skyline in that wild country.

The three smaller wolves that had chased the caribou edged out of some rocks and joined the big boy, which I guessed was Alec's "old man wolf." Those three were nearly as large as the average full-grown Minnesota wolf, which is around eighty pounds, but in comparison with the big dog-wolf you could see they were "young 'uns," about seven or eight months old.

Pretty soon two other adult wolves, a cut smaller than the big boy, appeared on the ridgeline. One was a male; I saw him use a boulder as a scent station. The other looked like a female, probably the mother of the cubs.

After a few minutes the big boy started down the slope alone. The three cubs followed him a rod or so, but he turned his head and looked at them and they went back to the crest. Whether by a growl or snarl or some other sign, he plainly had given them orders to go back and stay put. Unlike foxes, where the vixen alone takes the cubs out and teaches them to hunt, both wolf parents cooperate in teaching their young to take care of themselves.

At a casual jog trot, occasionally breaking into the leisurely pacing gait which the wolf has but the dog hasn't, the big fellow dropped down the hillside toward the caribou. He made no effort whatever to keep them from seeing him but trotted along in the wide open.

When he was about a hundred yards from the herd, he walked out on a low rock outcropping, sat down on his tail and looked around casually, as though he had no interest whatever in those caribou.

"He aims to take one," Alec said. "Mebbe that'll draw the bear out."

What he meant was that the rogue bear had been robbing those wolves day after day and living high on the proceeds of their hunting. It seemed to have some uncanny knowledge of where and when they made a kill, and it would go there, drive them away and have their caribou for itself. That was what Alec was hoping for now, so that he wouldn't have to venture into that tangle. But he didn't know where the bear would appear and wasn't sure what move it would make. In spite of its shaggy bulk and the dumb look in its little pig-eyes, the big brown can charge a person at an amazing speed, and it's one of the craftiest animals outdoors when it wants to be.

After the big dog-wolf had let the caribou see him and get a little used to him, he jogged on down to the moraine flat. Then began one of the most remarkable exhibitions of stalking skill and shrewd maneuvering that I've ever observed from any creature. I had seen wolves use this same general technique; in fact it's their common stalking method; but I'd never watched an instance so clear-cut and masterly.

Keeping to that leisurely trot and pace, the wolf first

made a circuit entirely around the pasture flat, staying a few rods from the outside fringe of the herd. The caribou nearest him would stop browsing and watch him closely as he passed them, and a few individuals moved in toward the center of the moraine, but there was no fright, no stampeding. As plain as day, the wolf's apparent lack of interest in the caribou deceived them into believing they weren't being stalked. But all the time, as he loafed along so innocently, he was not only lulling their fears but looking them over with an expert eye and deciding which one he'd try for.

After making that leisurely circuit, the wolf jogged out across the middle of the flat. There the caribou were thickest, and they opened up a wide swath to let him through. That is, the animals he headed toward would trot aside thirty or forty yards, watch him till he was past, then fall to browsing again.

For a good twenty minutes the wolf kept cutting back and forth through the herd at different angles, with the caribou paying him less and less attention. Now and then he would stop and look around, make use of a boulder as a scent station or scratch a belly flea with a hind leg. Altogether it was a bang-up job of acting. You see these play-acting stratagems very widely outdoors, such as the wing-broken killdeer, the dying sandpiper, the "dead" possum, the coyote's several cunning tricks; but that wolf's show of indifference to the caribou was a little more recondite than any of these, and he carried it through to the end without one false move.

As I watched him I was forcefully reminded of the term "loafer wolf." That's what the Great Plains wolf was often called in the days of the buffalo herds. I'd read various modern explanations of that term and none of them seemed really to explain it. But after I'd seen some tundra wolves hunting caribou—how they loaf around and through a herd like a person who has nothing to do and all day to do it—I knew beyond any question why the buffalo wolf was called the "loafer." It's the exact right word.

All this time the other wolves stayed up on the ridge-line, silently watching. Even the frisky cubs sat down and kept quiet. From first to last there was no yelping around, no massed onslaught by the pack, no "relay" maneuvers or other complicated battle strategy.

To be sure, wolves do occasionally indulge in these fancy tactics. They do it, I am convinced, mostly out of exuberance and mostly in the fall, when hunting is lush and easy. But it isn't their common way of getting food. When you consider that nearly one wolf out of two, by demonstrable figures, perishes from starvation, you realize that as a rule they just don't dare go chasing healthy animals around over the landscape for hours on end. They've got to make their kills with the least possible expenditure of strength and energy. This "loafer" technique is far and away their most efficient method, and it's the technique they use whenever they possibly can.

Just how the big dog-wolf picked out the animal he considered the easiest to take—this I couldn't figure out and Alec didn't know either. Out on the tundra you'll often see a wolf chase a small band of caribou a few hundred yards, then switch off and chase another band. He's merely testing them to see if there's a sick animal among them, or a calf that can't keep up. But when he selects a caribou without this test running, he evidently can detect signs of weakness, age, disease or other impairment which humans can't see.

Almost every time when you examine an adult caribou that wolves have killed, you'll find that it was either an old "gummer" (its teeth mostly gone), or weakened by excessive botfly grubs, or suffering from one of the various forms of exostosis that are common among caribou.

Pretty soon we saw that the wolf was narrowing down and focusing his attention on a little knot of caribou, nine or ten of them, at the upper side of the herd. This small bunch contained the undersized calf I mentioned, and I felt sure he was intending to go for it. But no. When he struck, it was at an adult animal, a medium-sized bull.

To us this caribou looked as healthy, strong and speedy as any in the herd. But the wolf knew different. He knew his business.

Still jogging along leisurely, he approached this little knot at an oblique angle, as though intending to go on past. Suddenly—and I mean suddenly—he whirled and plunged at the small group. All the other animals got under way fast and went streaking off in a wide semicircle, across the swale and back down into the main herd. But the bull caribou that the wolf had picked was slow to get going. Cut off from the others, it headed up the swale. It had good open ground and should have run that wolf bowlegged. But something was the matter with it. In that straight, all-out run the wolf gained on it swiftly, caught it after only a three hundred yard race and brought it down. There was a short struggle and that was the end of it.

I heard Alec mutter, *"Akosaneh, meesum!"* which meant something like "A fine job, cousin." Forgetting about his half-ton, two hundred dollar bear, he had been watching the stalk as intently as I. It was only a small lapse on his part, but when you're dealing with a big brown that's grown vicious and disrespectful of man, any lapse at all may cost you plenty.

If a person hasn't studied wolves very much or thought about their relationship with game animals, the question of whether they take their prey one way instead of another may seem inconsequential. But this isn't so. It is important to realize that wolves can't ordinarily catch a healthy animal and don't usually make their kills at random, but deliberately search through a herd and select the weak, old, sick or unfit individuals. It means that wolves prey mostly on undesirable breeding stock; that in reasonable numbers wolves don't harm or deplete a herd but actually improve it by keeping it at a high level of vigor and fertility.

This general principle is not limited to wolves and their relationship with game herds. It is becoming widely recognized in regard to other wildlife problems. For instance, a herd of deer on, say, an island, where they are protected from natural predators and from hunting, will in the course of just a decade not only decrease in numbers but tend to become small and runty and so lacking in vigor that they winter-kill very badly. As another instance, Lake A and Lake B are identical in all respects, except that Lake A is posted and Lake B is heavily fished. Strange as it may seem to the layman, Lake B will have many more fish and better fish than the lake which is posted.

But to get back to my story. After the big wolf made his kill, the other wolves came rushing down the slope. But that was all I got to see of them. Things began happening like that well-known basket of firecrackers.

A sudden grunt from Alec was my first intimation of anything wrong. When I jerked around, he was getting to his feet and whipping up his gun. Looking past him, I saw the rogue bear, down the slope and only about forty-five yards away. It had stopped and reared up on its hind legs and was squinting at us in that nest of rocks, as though puzzled by creatures that seemed to be composed of nothing but hats and heads.

Evidently the bear had moved out to the upper edge

of its lay-up, caught our wind and came sneaking up the slope to do us in. It had covered two-thirds of the distance without our hearing or seeing it. If it had kept on coming, if it hadn't got puzzled and stopped and reared up for a look-see, Alec and I might have been in for a lively time of it.

As it was, the brute not only made a target as big as an outhouse, but by rearing up it exposed itself to a heart-shot. Alec gave it to him three times, and all three shots were bang into the middle of the left ribs. The terrific smash of that one-two-three punch toppled the bear over backwards, and it rolled a little ways down the slope, lashing around with its front paws and plowing furrows with its tremendous claws.

It wasn't very much good after that. But it did get up and try to come on. With those three big slug holes through its chest and blood gushing out in streams, it actually got to its feet and started up that slope to demolish us. A brown bear, the Indians say, has got lots of *seepnak*. That means it hangs onto life strongly, is very hard to kill.

Alec said, "It's done for," and didn't waste any more ammunition on it. But we waited till it was good and dead before we went down there.

As we looked at the huge, shaggy, musky-smelling thing and realized we'd better be hitting down the long slope for our boat, I thought about the wolf family and how the bear had been robbing them, and I remarked: "This will sort of settle their score with this fellow. He fattened up on their caribou; now they'll eat him. Or will they?"

Alec grunted, "*Tahpwah!*" which meant something like, "You bet your boots." He said: "Bear meat is strong, sweet. You'll hear 'em. Tonight. From across at the camp. The young 'uns'll be eating and *yeolping* around." He was feeling mighty good, mostly about that two hundred dollars. He kicked the dead rogue bear and gave the wolves that old cook-shanty yell—"Come 'n git it!"

CATSKILL ADVENTURES

Circus on the Hillside

ONE sunny afternoon in late May I went back into a dairy-farm hill region to pursue my study of groundhog feeding habits. But shortly after I got there I spotted a litter of fox cubs playing around outside their den on a long, open slope, and that was the end of my groundhog study for that afternoon.

My outdoors partner, Smoky, a gentle and superbly intelligent black Doberman pinscher, was along, and I said to him: "We'll angle over there and slip up easy-like, and have us some fun teasing those little scalawags."

Smoke knew what I meant. We'd teased fox cubs before. Every spring we had some good times locating fox dens, watching fox family life and amusing ourselves with the hooligan cubs. This is an item which anybody who lives in fox country could well add to his spring and early-summer repertoire. It merely takes a little know-how, which I'll indicate here, plus maybe binoculars, and a camera if you're a shutterbug.

We climbed over a rock fence and headed out across the field. The pasture grass was only ankle high, and with no rocks, brush, gullies or cover of any sort, the stalking job wasn't a particularly easy one. Wild fox cubs, when they sense danger, are mighty skittish things. But they have their blind spots and you can get up close if you work it right. In approaching those cubs we had to rely entirely on keeping down wind, making no noise and moving in a certain slow, flowing way, with no quick or abrupt motions.

There were five in that litter, seven or eight weeks old and about the size of small cats. Keeping within a rod or two of the den, they were sunning themselves, scratching fleas, wallowing in the apron of dirt in front of the burrow, fighting, chasing one another, making clumsy efforts to stalk some blackbirds, and nibbling around in patches of clover and grass. Incidentally, fox cubs eat a great deal of green stuff. Not as a laxative but as food. They are fond of blue grass, clover, alfalfa, and particularly fond of the meadow sorrels, which are tart with oxalic acid.

A couple of hundred feet away I stopped a few minutes and studied the five cubs with my binoculars. I knew at once whose whelps they were. Back in that range I'd several times seen a trim, honey-colored vixen among the reds. In most places this color, merely a phase of the common red, is quite rare but in that section of the Catskill foothills I'd met with it again and again. Four of the cubs had the usual drab-brown fox-pup fuzz, but the fifth was honey-colored, almost golden. So I knew this litter had been whelped by the handsome yellowish vixen I'd been seeing.

As I went on toward the den, I wondered why I didn't see or hear anything of the two parent foxes. Nearly always they try their level best to lure or scare an intruder away from their young. The male will flash out of a thicket right in front of a dog's nose and draw him off, and the vixen will flit around from cover to cover letting loose little volleys of barks and throaty *ky-yee-yacks* which she imagines are very frightening. But I didn't see hide nor hair of either parent fox, and I concluded they were taking a siesta in a woods at the bottom of the slope.

When Smoke and I were about a hundred feet away, the cubs finally spotted us, as I could tell by their actions. But they didn't get scared and pop into the hole. In bright sunshine the eyesight of the young fox, like that of the young wolf and coyote, seems to be rather dim, and they don't rely on it much. Largely they depend on their sense of smell and their hearing. Particularly their smell. If you let them wind you, ordinarily you can't get closer than a couple of hundred feet. But those five couldn't smell Smoke and me, and my careful approach had them puzzled rather than scared.

Slow and cautious, we kept edging closer and closer— seventy-five feet, fifty, thirty-five; and I wondered how much longer this would go on. The cubs had quit fighting and messing around, and were giving me all their attention, not being able to see much of Smoke. It was comical the way they sat down more or less in a row, all five of them, and watched me fixedly, with a mixture of uneasiness and bug-eyed, kindergarten curiosity.

I could feel their tension mounting, and when I knew they were about to panic, I stopped and stood quiet, looking at them. Being a person who likes facts and figures, I made a mark in the dirt with my boot toe and later stepped off the distance from me to where they'd sat. It was between twenty and twenty-one feet! That's the closest I remember slipping up on a fox litter, but usually you can get up to thirty-five or forty feet if you keep quiet, keep down wind, move with a slow sway, and if the old foxes don't come around and sound off.

We must have stood there five minutes, Smoke and myself, eying that row of wild imps and getting the eye in return. When I made like a mouse, with pursed lips, five sets of little sharp ears would wiggle interestedly and five little heads would cock this way and that.

Finally Smoke, a superb stalker himself, edged out from behind me and stood against my leg. The honey-colored cub—I was calling him Spunky by now—made a sudden dash in our direction. The only way I could figure this was that the cub thought Smoke was one of its parents, bringing in a rabbit or young woodchuck. It got halfway to us before discovering its mistake. Like a flash it whirled around, streaked back to the den and popped in, and the other four went popping after it—*zip, zip, zip.*

I walked back across the fields to a draw where I'd shot a woodchuck for stomach-analysis purposes, and brought the carcass back to the den. After scenting up the burrow entrance with it, I pegged the carcass to the ground ten feet away. Then Smoke and I went off and sat down, about fifty feet from the hole, and waited for our homemade circus to start.

If you think we had to wait very long, you don't know young foxes. They're always half-starved, however well the parents provide, and on top of that they're the scrappingest, fightingest things outdoors. In less than five minutes Spunky came easing out of the den, sniffed around and approached the groundhog carcass. Then the others, all steamed up over the smell of blood and fresh meat, came boiling out. And that's when the fun began.

Immediately there was a big fight. Instead of setting to and eating, those five little toughies set to and had a roundhouse battle—a noisy, free-for-all, Pier Six brawl, along with a furious snarling, hissing, *kaa-acking* and yipping. Nobody fought anybody else in particular. A would be chewing on B, while B would be wading into D, and D would have E by the leg, while C would be in the middle biting everybody. Smoke was sitting against my elbow wagging his tail and watching, and if that dog wasn't laughing at the fracas I'd like to know what he was doing.

Wild fox cubs, high-strung to the point of being mildly explosive, are incessant fighters. In a litter of wolf cubs there'll be a certain amount of scrapping at first, but then one individual emerges as boss, and that's the end of it. Besides, it isn't wolf nature to fight much among themselves. But a litter of fox cubs will stage one of these brawls, and somebody wins, and then ten minutes later everything comes unstuck and they do it all over again. In addition to ordinary biting, slashing and chewing, they have a favorite trick, which an adult fox often uses in fighting another fox. They will dart in, whirl, throw their tail and hindquarters into their opponent's face, and all he gets is a mouthful of hair. While he's getting that out of his teeth, they deliver a slash and duck back out again.

Our five little rascals made so much commotion that they woke up the dog-fox, who was napping down in the woods, as I'd surmised; and he came tearing up the slope to see what on earth was the matter with his brats. He was only a few yards from the den when he noticed Smoke and me. The sight of us sort of paralyzed him for a second or two—we were so close, on the wide-open slope. He was scared to death, and you'd think he would have turned in his tracks and bolted, which was the quickest way to get gone. But no. With a true parent instinct he made a swing on up towards us, ran between us and the cubs, and only then took off—floating out the slope with the swift, graceful ease of a swallow's flight.

I wondered where the vixen was and why she hadn't showed up. Almost always they are the first and foremost in guarding the den and young.

Evidently the dog-fox had flashed some unseen warning to the cubs, because they broke off their brawl and zipped into the burrow. But pretty soon they boiled back out again, and what did they do? Why, they started another fight. After maybe five minutes one of them came out the winner. I couldn't see why; he hadn't licked anybody that I'd noticed. But he went over and stood on top of the groundhog and was Boss. When one of the others would come too close to suit him, he'd arch his back like a cat, bare his fangs like a dog, make a horrible face and go *kaa-ack*—a sort of snarling, spitting, catlike cough that's hard to describe.

A friend had asked me to get him a young fox for a pet, so after Smoke and I had watched our circus twice around, I decided to try to capture one of the five, though they were considerably larger and older than a fox cub ought to be if you're going to make a really fine pet out of it. The one I wanted was that honey-colored Spunky.

I went down to the den—they popped into it, of course —and fixed a whipcord noose around the hole, tailed the cord out about twenty feet, and lay down flat on the ground. With this wrinkle you can usually snag a cub in ten to fifteen minutes. But it didn't work this time. I could hear the cubs barking around back in the hole but they wouldn't come out.

So I cut off a piece of groundhog meat, tied it to another length of cord, flipped it well back into the hole and lay down again to wait. I've pulled fox cubs right out of the burrow that way. You'll hear a commotion back in the hole, then a cub will latch onto the meat, and if you pull slow and easy and keep quiet you can sometimes draw them clear out of the den. But that wrinkle didn't work either. The little smarties knew I was around.

After trying a couple of other tricks and no dice, Smoke and I took up the groundhog carcass and sat down again up the slope, about seventy-five feet away. We had to wait quite a while, and I watched around the edge of the field and along the woods for the vixen. She should have showed up, and I knew definitely by now that something was wrong.

When the cubs finally came out, they began looking around for the groundhog. From their furious little scraps you'd think they were accusing one another of having swiped and hid it somewhere. They were mighty keen to find it and hunted all over, venturing farther and farther from the den. I watched Spunky, who was hunting down slope from the den, and when he was far enough away from it, I said:

"Go get him, Smoke. Careful now. He's a nice little fox and don't you hurt him."

Any creature that I pointed out and said it was a "nice little" such-and-such, Smoke positively wouldn't hurt. He knew I wanted it unharmed. I'm sure that if I had said to him, "That's a nice little hippopotamus," he would have tried his level best to get the beast down and hold it till I came. Besides this training and his extra-friendly nature, he had been raised with a fox-cub playmate and regarded foxes much as he regarded other dogs.

I gave him a shove and he took off down the slope. A couple of the other cubs, seeing they were cut off from the den, sank down on the ground and "froze," which is a typical reaction of many young animals in similar circumstances. Spunky lit out for the rock fence on the far side of the field. But his legs just weren't long enough yet, and in a few jumps Smoke caught him, got him down, put a paw on him and stood wagging his tail as though trying to reassure the little fellow that everything was all right.

While I was getting there the cub bit Smoke rather severely, with its needle-sharp teeth, but when I picked it up it made no attempt to bite me at all. Why this should be I don't know but I've noticed it many times. Till wild fox cubs get nearly half-grown you can handle them safely with bare hands.

It was quite a prize, this honey-colored cub. I crouched down there holding it, stroking it to still its panic, and looked the little thing over. However many times you've done this, you always notice something you've never observed before. Like all other fox cubs, this one was lean and gaunt, astonishingly light for its size, immaculately clean, and extremely high-tensioned, even after I'd gentled most of its panic away. A wild fox cub is the second most high-strung creature I know about. The shrew is the first. Holding a shrew in your hand is like holding a wad of electricity, and a fox cub isn't far behind.

Its eyes were the thing that got me. It would stare at Smoke, then turn its head slowly and stare at me, and for some reason it looked directly at my eyes. For a creature that size its eyes were large, and they were very expressive. The pupils were extra large, fawn-colored and roughly diamond-shaped. They had another quality which I can only describe as "bottomless." Looking into the eyes of a wild fox cub is an experience. Do it some time and you'll see what I mean. It's like looking into another world.

I took Spunky back up to the den and put him down on the apron of dirt. For a few moments he just squatted there, not realizing he was free. But then I gave him a nudge with my boot, and *zip!*—he was back into the den faster than a sliver of greased lightning.

I remember thinking, rather sorrowfully, that considering the high mortality among young foxes, this was the last that Smoke and I would ever see of the honey-colored little fellow. But it wasn't, as I'll tell you about when we come to it.

It was a good thing I didn't take Spunky home and give him to my friend. The cub was too big and too old and it would have wound up as one of those miserable creatures you see chained up or penned up, eating its heart out for the free wild life of its birthright. Such creatures aren't pets. They're prisoners. And soon they turn unnatural, all of them—sort of "stir crazy."

If you want a genuine fox pet, you must get it very young, preferably before its eyes are open. You should raise it by itself; that is, without any of its litter mates or an adult fox around. And you must expect to give it every bit as much training and care as you'd give to raising a good, mannerly, companionable dog. Most important, don't overfeed it. Keep it lean and light. If overfeeding is bad for a dog, it's fatal for a fox.

If you follow these simple recommendations, you can have a creature that's tame, friendly, homebound and thoroughly enjoyable, and that's also quite a unique pet. They get along fine with the household dog but strange dogs persecute them pretty badly. They are very markedly a "one-man dog," uneasy around strangers and always running to their master for protection or comfort. Far more than any dog, they like to nap in their master's lap or cuddle up at his feet. In this respect, as in others, they are somewhat catlike, as compared with a dog.

All the tall tales to the contrary, the fox is a bit dumb when you match him with a dog in ways that show up intelligence. In a few limited respects, such as stalking game or eluding capture, a fox is indeed sharper than a dog, but the general level of its intelligence is lower. If you are teaching the same tricks to a young dog and a young fox, as I have done, you quickly see that the fox gets tired of mental exertion much sooner than the dog and doesn't have the dog's versatility in meeting unfamiliar situations. All this, of course, is not to say that the fox is any dumbhead. Compared with other animals in the wild, it's a smart cookie. But compared with dogs—or wolves—it has to take a back seat.

When the vixen, in late March or early April, feels her whelping time approaching, she goes around and prepares not one den but several, usually by enlarging woodchuck burrows. One of these will be the whelping den. The others are for emergency use. If the main den becomes foul or some danger develops, the vixen will move her cubs to one of the emergency places.

A fox den is easily recognizable by one or more distinctive signs:

1) The main entrance is much larger than a groundhog would dig. The side holes of the burrow may or may not be enlarged.

2) Almost always the main entrance has a big, conspicuous apron of loose dirt. This serves the cubs as a dust wallow, which helps keep down their fleas and mites. With binoculars I've spotted these dirt aprons half a mile away.

3) If you slip up noiselessly and listen, you'll often hear the cubs scuffling and growling around back in the nest or lay-up chamber. When very tiny, the cubs mew not unlike kittens. A bit older, they have a diminutive bark. Sometimes you hear them fighting back in the nest.

4) After the cubs get to be about four weeks old, you'll usually see some bones, feathers, pieces of skin, dead mice, shrews, frogs, etc., around the hole.

5) The odor of fox dens is quite characteristic, and after you've smelled it a time or two you can recognize it readily. The odor is strong, somewhat musky but not unpleasant.

6) You can often spot the vixen standing guard over her young, from some high spot nearby. You don't often see the dog-fox. At the risk of starting an argument, I'll state that ordinarily the dog-fox doesn't do very much in the way of providing. If the hunting is lean, the dog may help out some, bringing his kill to within a few rods of the den, and the vixen taking it on in. But if the vixen can feed the family by herself, he puts in his time lying around on some sunny hillside, smoking a pipe and watching the clouds go sailing by. However, in an emergency the dog-fox can and sometimes will take over the entire job of feeding and rearing the young.

7) If you get near a fox den, under the right conditions, the vixen—very rarely the dog-fox—will let you know about it in no uncertain terms. This is the easiest and best way of all to locate a den with cubs. If the den is in the middle of a field, with no cover close, and if you approach in broad day, the vixen will usually lie low and keep quiet. But in a woods or a brushy situation, and in any situation during twilight or at night, the vixen will start barking and *ky-yee-yacking* if you get within several hundred yards of the place where she has her precious bairns. I've located dens many a time that way where I never would have suspected any litter of cubs if the vixen hadn't come and told me about it.

For the last ten or fifteen years foxes have been on the increase almost everywhere in the United States and Canada. The fur hasn't been fetching any price to speak of, and the bounties which have sprung up widely, ranging from one to four dollars, with an average of two dollars, aren't enough to make hunting and trapping profitable for the farm lad, who was always the great producer of fox pelts. A prime fox skin used to bring fifteen to twenty-five dollars. Now it brings a tenth of that; the lesser grades aren't worth skinning, stretching and shipping.

This terrific slump in fox peltry price is partly due to the swing in fashion away from the long-haired furs such as fox, raccoon and wolf. But mostly, it's said, the slump has been due to the fact that Russia has been dumping huge quantities of fox peltry onto the market in Europe and America, at incredibly low prices. At one time prime Grade A fox pelts from Russia were unloaded on the New York dock at sixty-five cents a pelt.

In spite of the increase in fox numbers, there are few places where the fox population has reached the pest level. Now and then rabies may break out among the foxes in a district, but this is rare, and the government field biologists do a splendid job in stamping out the disease. Poultry depredation, which is the commonest complaint against Reynard, is in reality usually slight and limited to certain individuals. The belief that the fox destroys great quantities of small game and birds hasn't been borne out by the extensive and authoritative studies made, chiefly the analyses of fox scats. The fox menu, considered around the seasons, does show a certain amount of rabbit, quail, small bird, very occasionally pheasant and grouse, but nothing like the amount so often charged.

The truth is that the adult fox is a confirmed mouser, and he will hunt mice almost to the exclusion of anything else, when he can. At pinch times, such as deep snow or crust, he can't mouse, and then he'll take whatever game he can find. But he prefers mice, and he hunts them long and assiduously. He captures all kinds of small rodents and insectivores—harvest mice, red-backs, deer mice, lemmings, voles, shrews, meadow mice and others; but the meadow mouse (*Microtus*) is his favorite, and he destroys prodigious numbers of them. Sometimes you are lucky enough to see a fox mousing in the daytime, and then you see a memorable exhibition of hunting skill. He will trot along soft-footed, stop suddenly, listen, pounce as much as ten feet at a mouse he cannot see, running along a hidden mouseway, and unerringly get his prey. A quick brain-bite, a crunch or two, and he's off after another.

A couple of weeks after my first visit, I went back to that den on the hillside and looked for my little scalawags. They were gone and there were cobwebs in the hole. We combed the woods below, Smoke and I, and hunted through half a dozen surrounding fields. But we couldn't find them, couldn't even find any fresh tracks or other signs of them, and I was afraid that some disaster had wiped them all out.

We did, though, find out why the honey-colored vixen hadn't showed up that day of our visit. Down in that patch of woods we came across the carcass of a fox hanging on an old barbed-wire fence. Somebody had shot the animal a full month ago and draped it over the wire. Nothing much was left except fur and bones, but the fur was a telltale honey color.

Along in the last of August I began going back into those woodchuck-infested hills a couple of times a week and eliminating the groundhogs in certain areas as part of a dispersion study I was making. One afternoon when I was sitting on a rock fence and Smoke was trotting along through some scattered briars down in the bottom, I happened to notice that a smallish fox was trailing him, keeping about five hundred feet behind. I lifted my glasses and looked, and blow me down, it was Spunky! He was about two-thirds grown now—in long pants, you might say—but the honey color was unmistakable.

I knew by now that something bad had happened to all the rest of that fox family, and I was surely glad that the handsome, gold-washed Spunky was still alive.

I watched him for quite a spell. There was no doubt he was following Smoke, keeping at a discreet distance, and I wondered what he was up to. It was something out of the ordinary, that was for sure. When a dog trails a fox, that's not news, but when a fox trails a dog, that *is*.

The next time I went back there, I kept my eye peeled. Sure enough, I saw Spunky again, trailing Smoke. After some head-scratching, I had an idea. We had been dispatching a considerable number of groundhogs back in there and leaving the carcasses after I had weighed and analyzed the stomach contents, and I wondered if that confounded young fox had caught on that by following us he could help himself to a royal feed.

I called Smoke in and we went over into the next field, where we shot a groundhog. Then we angled down to the small creek at the bottom of the long hillside, sat down behind a big sycamore tree and watched.

Pretty soon, exactly as I'd thought, Spunky went slipping out across that field and started to work on that groundhog windfall.

"Well, what d'you know!" I said to Smoke. "Can you beat that, fellow? And here I was saying, a while back, that a fox is sort of dumb!"

The New Look in Animal Homes

IT is said of us human beings that there's no place like home, and certainly this is doubly true for the small animals of our woods and fields.

Their homes serve all the purposes that ours do and other needs besides. It's their only shelter in vile weather, their nursery when their young are born, their refuge against pursuing enemies, their haven when they are sick or wounded, their lay-up place during the cold, foodless spells in winter. They don't have other recourses, as we do, such as hotels, clubs, hospitals, a friend's place, a summer cabin by a lake. Their one home is all they've got, and it's just a burrow in the ground.

A person might say: "Well, what's wrong with that? A burrow in the ground is all they ever did have, isn't it? It's their natural home and why isn't it all right?"

The answer to these questions is quite complex and too lengthy for us to go into here. But I will point out that most of our country is settled or semi-settled and that therefore conditions have vastly changed from what they were in the forest primeval or on the unbroken Great

Plains; that the original homes and shelters for so many small animals have been destroyed; that most of our wild animal species are fighting a losing battle and steadily diminishing in numbers, and need every help we can give them. And in no way can we help them more than in this matter of their homes.

Surprising as it may seem to the uninitiated, a "natural den" is a miserable home for animals. In the first place, it's not their "natural" den. Their natural homes have been destroyed and they use the ground burrow only because it's all that's available to them. In the second place, it's not the snug, safe, healthy place that most people imagine. On the contrary, it's dank, dirty, vermin-infested and disease-breeding, especially with rabbits. It floods easily, and in clay soils most holes have puddles in them. And the blind pockets in burrows often make them a death trap when the fox, weasel or hungry mink goes from hole to hole looking for its dinner.

Most ground burrows are dug by woodchucks, and these are notoriously poor home architects. In the course of studying woodchuck habits I have excavated many holes and probe-explored scores of others, and I will say that hardly one in half a dozen is even minimumly fit as an animal abode, and none of them is really good. In another place I go into detail about the woodchuck and the wretched home it engineers. Here I will merely remark that these "natural dens" are so bad that an important step in small-animal conservation on an area is to go around and plug up and eliminate as many as possible of the old, unhealthy ground holes. In other words, they are worse than nothing at all.

Many years ago the Department of Agriculture developed a device to eliminate pest animals, chiefly rabbits, around orchards, gardens and truck farms. Since the device was used for eradication, they called it the "shelter trap." As a trap it worked amazingly well and had many advantages, which I will mention in a minute, over other methods of trapping. But then it was discovered that since small animals took to it so readily and *used it as a home*, it could be employed in situations where the fur-bearers and small game animals needed protection, needed something better than the ground burrows available; and so in the course of time the device became known as the "shelter den."

Basically a shelter den is nothing more than two or three lengths of tile and a box. In terms of the ordinary burrow, the tile represents the hole or tunnel, and the box is the lay-up chamber or nest. The top of the box is hinged or otherwise lidded so that a person can look in whenever he wants to.

Operating this device is quite simple. The operator inserts in the tile a stick with a disc on the end to keep the occupant from running out. Then he opens the top, and if the animal is an undesirable he can dispatch it with a .22 or capture it in a bag. If it is a welcome occupant, he can leave it undisturbed, put the lid back on and go along.

There are certain situations and times when animals must be trapped, either to eliminate pests or to remove excess animals to another location or for other reasons. And then, to be realistic about it, there is a lot of fur-bearer trapping going on and this promises to continue for a long time yet. So I intend, here, to point out the advantages of the "shelter den" as a trap, if and when a person must trap.

1) It is *humane*. This fact will be obvious to anybody who knows the unpleasant actualities of the ordinary trap-line, especially where the cruel steep trap is employed. An animal taken in the shelter-den way is dispatched with an absolute minimum of pain or panicky thrashing around.

2) It is *easy, quick, convenient*. In these respects no other method—steel trap, deadfall, snare, gun or whatnot —approaches it. I myself have had considerable experience with control trapping and have seen a great deal of fur-path trapping, and the shelter-den method is easily the best of all. There is no painstaking trap setting, baiting, scenting. Your trapline isn't getting loused up all the time by varying weather, snows or ice conditions. Nor do you have your traps stolen. And you don't have to run your line at daybreak and every day. Any slack hour of the day will do, or you can skip it altogether.

3) It is highly *selective*, whereas most of the other methods aren't selective at all. For instance, a steel trap catches anything that happens along, indiscriminately— the kit animal, the *wrong* animal, the female with young,

the animal with unprime fur; and it will maim others that tear free or gnaw themselves loose. A state game commissioner writes me, "Only one animal in three that are taken in ordinary traps should have been taken, for the good of the peltry supply," and a brief visit to any wild-fur house will surely show you the truth of this. Using the shelter-den way, a person takes only prime, grade A peltry. He lets the kits go, to become prime grade A the next year.

Such are the main advantages of the shelter den as a trap. But you probably aren't much interested in that, and neither am I, so we'll go on to its real use and value—its function in sheltering, controlling and increasing small-animal life.

First, I'll tell you how to construct a shelter den. My suggestions are a composite of my own experience and the recommendations of game conservators, the biology field experts and others who have worked with it.

A good shelter den takes a couple of hours to make and may cost a dollar or two. But the job, once done, lasts a lifetime and is a permanent addition to one's farm or summer place or cabin in the woods.

The tile runway or tunnel ought to be not less than four feet long and not more than six. It ought to tilt slightly down, for drainage, and should be covered with rocks for anchorage and also with soil to seal out any light. Where weasels and mink are a problem, dens primarily for rabbits should have two runways, one on each side of the lay-up box, so that the rabbits can escape when the predator comes calling.

For animals like rabbits, possums and skunks, the best diameter size of the tile is, in my opinion, six inches. Sometimes you will see smaller tile recommended, the idea being to keep out foxes, cats and driver dogs. However, if your animals have too much of a tight fit coming and going, they won't use the den as freely as otherwise. My remedy is to drive down two properly spaced stakes at the entrance of the tile. This screens out the marauders mentioned above but leaves the rest of the runway comfortably large.

For the lay-up chamber or lair a wooden box does very well, except that it doesn't last. Metal is better, stone or concrete the best of all. For several of my dens I was lucky enough to secure some hollow concrete squares that were just about perfect. The lids I made of wood, and I used felt stripping to seal out the light. This is an important point. A sealed den is warmer in winter, cooler in summer, and animals feel more secure in a refuge that is pitch dark.

These lay-up chambers should be ample in size. They shouldn't be high; fifteen inches is plenty for this dimension. But they should be at least fifteen inches, preferably eighteen, on a side, to provide two square feet or more of floor area. You will find that after animals start using a shelter den it will be occupied by several individuals. I made the mistake at first of having boxes that provided only one square foot. I remember one occasion when I opened the lid of a small box and saw four full-grown cottontails cram-jammed into that little space. Possums are sociable animals and will bunch up, sometimes four or five. Skunks are very sociable. Litter mates stay together through the fall and winter, and I have known of instances where two litters—a dozen or more skunks—wintered in the same den.

At times I've had people complain that they constructed shelter dens and then animals wouldn't use them. When you go and take a look, you nearly always find that the den wasn't properly made or was badly placed. As likely as not, the person just threw down a couple of tiles on top of the ground and stuck a box over the end any old way. For good results the tile must be anchored and covered, and both it and the lay-up chamber must be reasonably lightproof. Also, the more natural-looking the den and surroundings, the better.

As for location, don't place a shelter den where animals never go. Locate it just inside a woods edge, along a brushy rock fence, in a thicket—in cover of some kind. And give a thought to the proximity to water, food supply and other desiderata.

When the job is done right and still animals seem to avoid the den, don't be disappointed. Just wait. Usually the den has to be there a while and sort of age. You may have no customers for several weeks. A couple of my best

dens went all summer and late into the fall without customers.

By way of illustration, let me tell you about a particular den, NY-14, which I set up on a briar slope over-
looking a little lake. My primary purpose was to see what
time in the fall the new crop of rabbits, plentiful on that
slope, would start using the shelter. As things turned out,
the den was in so much demand by other tenants that I
never did find out what I wanted to know. At that den,
anyhow.

We constructed it, Smoke and I, near the end of May
and then stayed away from it for a month, as a person
should. On our first visit we found it unused. On our second visit, in mid-July, we found it occupied by a big, fat,
sleepy possum. I lifted him out by the tail, lugged him off
and deposited him in a brush pile. But on our next trip,
there was that confounded possum again. That time we
took him in the car and put him out in a woods several
miles distant, and hoped that now the rabbits would have
a chance.

On our next visit, Smoke took a whiff at the tile entrance, then backed off about twenty feet and began digging. I knew that this meant skunks. Out of sad experience, Smoke knew that skunks were not to be monkeyed
with. Yet his instincts, when he'd come upon a hole with
skunks in it, would prompt him to dig around after them.
So—a goofy compromise—he would back off a rod or so
and just start digging.

When I warily looked into NY-14, I saw that two half-grown skunks had moved in. They stayed there for several weeks, till finally I knocked them out with chloroform one day and hustled them far enough away that they didn't come back. On our visit after that, Smoke got very excited, and I wondered "What now?" When I opened the top, out squirted a mink. Not, if you please, just any old kind of a mink but absolutely nothing less than a platinum blue! I learned later that a batch of these had escaped from a new mink farm a couple of miles away but at the moment I was flabbergasted no end.

So it went, there at NY-14, all summer and fall—more skunks, a raccoon, a stray woodchuck, occasionally a rabbit, till finally a pair of possums moved in during early December, and I let them have it for the winter. The moral is that a well-located and properly constructed den never goes begging for occupants. The trouble is just the opposite; you have more applicants than you can shake a stick at. Animals know a good thing when they find it; and that safe refuge, that warm, dry home, is their idea of a good thing.

But easily the most popular and populated of all my shelter dens was the one I made for a little neighbor friend, the Monkey Pup. When he was only three, he used to go along with Smoke and me sometimes on our rounds, and nothing would do but that he should have a shelter den of his "really own." So Smoke and I made him one, in a patch of pines just back of his house, as a present on his fourth birthday. All winter it was a daily routine with him to equip himself as for a safari, each morning, and go out there and look in.

Providentially no skunks came. His guests were mostly rabbits. But Smoke and I heard wondrous tales about lions and "taggers" and suchlike, back at that shelter den —completely eclipsing anything that our own shelter dens drew. Then one morning he came flying back to the house, bug-eyed and stuttering, and reported:

"P-p-possums! H-h-unnerds 'n' h-h-hunnerds of p-pos-sums!"

He wasn't so far wrong, at that. During the night a mother possum had moved in, with her batch of young. They were about the size of deer mice, and so many that we never did get an accurate count. We figured one to the inch, all the way from her tail to her ears, and called it fifteen or sixteen, and let it go at that.

The Whistle Pig Plays It Safe

THE woodchuck population of the United States and Canada is slightly prodigious—around *half a billion*. Only a few species of birds and animals have managed to hold their own as our country was settled up, and of these the woodchuck is easily the champion. In fact, it has more than held its own. It is several times as numerous as when America was virgin wildland, and in most regions it is still on the increase.

Now this poses a pretty question: What does this unfavored creature, slow of foot, heavy of body and not exactly nimble in the brain—just what does it have that accounts for its spectacular success?

Most creatures with strong survival powers show some definite superiority, like the plover's swift grace of wing, the fox's super-keen nose, the tortoise's built-in armor, the otter's artistry as a fisherman. But the woodchuck not only lacks any such helpful specialty but is saddled with several handicaps that would sink the ordinary animal.

It's a sort of Nature whodunit, this "Case of the

Abounding Chuck," and the solution isn't easy to come by. You sleuth around digging into the woodchuck's private life; you come up with explanations and then sadly discover that they don't really explain; you run into flatly contradictory evidence and get baffled no end. But finally the puzzle does clear up and there it is, the odd, surprising answer to the riddle.

Before I get accused of being biased against the chuck, I want to say that personally I am quite fond of it, for all its shortcomings. It has occupied a big and pleasant niche in my outdoors life. The first pet I ever had was a tiny chuck, Wizzy—I was four years old and Wizzy four weeks—and I've raised many a one since. For me the sharp, diminuendo whistle of the woodchuck connotes the sunny farmlands of the Sangamon, the cathedral quiet of a deep Ozark woods, the rugged splendor of the Liard Rockies. On a thousand summer evenings I have gone out after the day's work and studied the chuck's feeding habits, made populations counts and otherwise used it as an excuse for being abroad at that magic hour. But the truth is that in some respects the chuck doesn't compare too favorably with other wild creatures, and I must try to set down that truth here as accurately as I know how.

To begin with, the woodchuck—or groundhog, chuck, marmot, whistle pig, yellow-belly, rock pig, rock chuck, rock beaver, *siffleur* and still other names—is a ground-squirrel, an overgrown cousin of the chipmunk and gopher. Our second biggest rodent, it averages twelve to fifteen pounds for the Eastern chuck and twenty pounds or better for the hoary marmot of the far-North Rockies. The common chuck (*Monax*) ranges out to the Great Plains in the United States but in Canada it extends clear west to the Pacific and north to Alaska. The yellow-belly (*Flaviventris*) is mostly Western and Southwestern. The hoary marmot (*Caligata*) occurs from Idaho north to the Arctic.

Any burrowing creature, whether animal, snake or insect, tends to be round in cross section, and so the groundhog is somewhat barrel-bodied as compared with the deep-chested wolf or a streamlined fish. Its short, stout legs are good digging equipment but poor for running. One noteworthy feature about the chuck is its big, ivory-chisel incisors, the lower ones measuring as much as *three inches* from root to tip. Another special feature is the woodchuck eye, which protrudes slightly above the top edge of the flat skull and makes a low-grade periscope, enabling the chuck to watch an enemy without exposing itself.

But these few favorable adaptations are more than offset by gross bodily disadvantages, which make the chuck slow and awkward. So, adaptation doesn't explain its huge success and we have to look elsewhere.

The changing environment as the country was settled up is sometimes cited as the reason for the chuck's great increase. Let's see if that might be the answer to our puzzle.

In deep-woods regions, like the Ozarks of south central Missouri, sample counts of groundhogs show that the chuck population in thick forest is quite low. The figure varies a lot but it's on the order of one chuck for every two to five acres. By contrast, the density in open farmland may be as high as two or three chucks per acre, or roughly ten times as much as in heavy woods. Available food is the big factor. This means that the original forest, which extended from the Atlantic Coast out to the buffalo plains, wasn't nearly as good a chuck habitat as the fields, pastures, orchards and cut-over hill land that came later.

Also, in that vanished American forest the woodchuck had many enemies. The Indian, wolf and panther were the three worst, but others were the coyote, bobcat and wolverine. The fox, eagle and large hawk can't handle adult chucks though they prey considerably on the young. In badger country old Dig Boy is at present the chuck's most serious natural enemy.

That the Indian was a great groundhog eater is attested by the large amount of woodchuck bones in camp-site refuse heaps and by other evidence. Near Rocky Mountain House in Alberta I once heard a Chippewa (Ojibway) remark that a fieldful of chucks was better than a field of potatoes. Later an authority on Indian lore told me that this was an old Chippewa saying, dating back to the time the Chippewas were an Eastern people, and that most of the tribes of the East had a similar saying. Altogether it is probable that the Red Man ate a great deal more groundhog meat than he did venison.

With the settling up of the country, the groundhog's

meager woods-fare of leaves and bark was replaced by the lush grasses and crops of the open fields, and at the same time its chief enemies all over its continent-wide range were either eliminated or greatly reduced in numbers. On the surface it would seem that these two potent facts explain the tremendous success of the chuck tribe. A good many observers have taken this for granted, and for a long while so did I. But when you look deeper you see that this explanation is a sort of booby trap for the unwary naturalist. A whole raft of questions raise their embarrassing heads. For instance:

Nearly always an increase in the numbers of a species is met by an increase of old enemies or the addition of new ones, but the chuck circumvented this natural law—how? The change of habitat from forest to field proved nearly fatal to many animals of comparable nature but to the chuck it was good luck—why?

The answer to these questions is that the woodchuck had something special, something which enabled it to take advantage of its radically changed environment. So, we are right back where we started—what *is* this hidden asset by which the chuck outdistanced its fellow creatures?

The woodchuck's year cycle has several unique phases and we might take a look at them and see if we come up with any clues.

Along about mid-November the groundhog, waddling fat, holes up and hibernates. The adults, which merely have to fatten up, go in first. The young, which have to attain growth besides laying on fat, go in about two weeks later than the adults. Other animals make themselves warm and adequate winter nests but this would be nonsense with the chuck. At most it carries in a few leaves—which as often as not it doesn't use! Typically it simply walls itself up in a side pocket, plumps down on the bare dirt and starts pounding the ear.

This hibernal sleep is very profound. Most people to whom you show a comatose chuck swear that the critter is dead. The faint, slow pulse and infrequent, shallow breathing are hard to detect without instruments, and the chuck feels stone cold because its body temperature is only about fifty degrees. In the laboratory this temperature can be taken down almost to freezing without apparent harm to the chuck.

It is conventional to say that the groundhog hibernates for five months. Actually the period is much shorter. In the region between the southern Catskills and northern New Jersey, I have kept strict records on this for eleven years, and the average hibernation period has been three and a half months. The main emergence usually takes place during the last week in February or the first week in March. My records indicate a curious fact. The *spring weather* doesn't noticeably affect the emergence date. Chucks will come out in rather severe cold and wallow around in the snow. It's the weather of the *preceding fall* that determines their awakening in the spring. For instance, if a fall is mild and chucks go in late, with maybe a bit of extra fat, they'll come out a little later in the spring than usual, regardless of the weather at that time.

The males wake up a few days earlier than the females and go prowling around from den to den, looking for a mate. In a light snow you will sometimes track a male for three quarters of a mile. They clean out and enter most of the dens they come across, and they engage in clumsy but gory fights with other males they encounter. Mating usually takes place inside the burrow. There is evidence that in at least some instances mating occurs while the female is still comatose.

The Groundhog Day myth has it that the woodchuck comes out on the second of February, takes a look at the weather and goes back in for a second sleep if it sees its shadow. Although this date is much too early for the awakening, except in the southern range, this myth has considerable truth to it. Once awakened, the chuck doesn't lapse back into the true hibernal sleep again, but it doesn't come out much for a month or more, after the brief mating flurry is over. The weather is usually inclement, the chuck appetite hasn't built up yet and there's little food anyhow, so it stays in its den most of the time, in a normal sleep. Let the rabbit frolic around all night if it wants to; let the coon and fox indulge their spring madness; let the crows tumble and toss in the gusty March sky, and the peepers burst their throats piping the spring in—all that is foolishness to the unhumorous chuck.

With a litter average of four and with only one litter a

year, the woodchuck has a low reproduction rate, especially so in a family (*Rodentia*) noted for fecundity. Rabbits and squirrels produce several times as many young per season. So, in this important matter the chuck is at serious disadvantage. Nor is this handicap made up for by extra maternal care. A week after their eyes are open the young start toddling outside and nibbling at green stuff, and soon thereafter they are weaned. A few weeks later they are driven out of the nursery, disperse, and take up solitary lives.

A young chuck a few weeks old is bright, active and a cute little thing. They remain lightfooted and agile for a month or so after the dispersion. They scrabble around over rocks nimbly and climb trees readily, and during this period you can readily see their blood kinship with the terrestrial squirrels.

But all too quickly they grow away from this ancestral type, as most young creatures do, and with the chuck this is a sad development. Chucks are such incessant eaters that by mid-July, when the young weigh three or four pounds, they have become slow and stolid. Frequently you walk up on half-grown chucks so paunch-heavy they are all but helpless. Sometimes a chuck weighing four pounds will show a stomach-content weight of three quarters of a pound! A man with forty or fifty pounds of food in him wouldn't be very active either.

After the first hard freeze in the fall, the chuck's hibernation instincts come into play. If you watch carefully at this time, you'll often see a curious little bobtailed chuck migration. Their summer dens, located in the open fields to be in the midst of the food supply, may not be suitable as winter quarters. So, woodchucks that have summered in a lush bottoms field will often leave the flat land towards the end of October and seek dens on a nearby brushy hillside. The chief reason for this seems to be that the lowland burrows might flood during the winter and drown them. Another reason is that when they emerge in the spring there is little green stuff in the fields and for a time they eat mostly bark and twigs of squat shrubbery.

There is a hunter's axiom that the brush groundhog goes in later and comes out earlier than the field groundhog. Nine times out of ten it's one and the same chuck.

The chief feature about the year cycle of the woodchuck is this hibernation business. Superficially this may look like an advantage—sleeping away the cold months in safe and secure oblivion. In reality hibernation exacts certain penalties which more than wipe the advantage out.

One of these penalties is the groundhog's food needs. Size for size, the chuck is the most tremendous eater of all our animals, exceeding even the notorious, high-strung shrew. Ordinarily an adult chuck feeds four times a day in late spring, three times daily during the summer and fall, and seldom does it stow away less than a pound of green stuff at a feeding. The average is somewhat over a pound. *Two-pound stomachs* crop up now and then in your records. And remember that it eats not once a day but up to four times. My summary figures on stomach weights indicate that a chuck will consume an equivalent of forty per cent of its own weight daily. That's as though an average-sized man would eat sixty pounds of food a day!

One time last summer a farmer friend phoned me that the groundhogs in one of his fields had all gone crazy and would I come and see what. It was quite a sight. In the middle of a large field from which he had just taken an ensilage crop, a dozen or more chucks were rushing around aimlessly and frantically, like the proverbial chicken with its head off. I'd seen this sight before and knew what the trouble was. The chucks were half-famished and in a mild panic. The farmer had cut the crop low and removed it cleanly, and they couldn't find enough to eat. In that same field a rabbit or prairie dog would have lived fat and sassy.

This big food requirement is a bad handicap to the chuck even in summer. In winter the chuck would starve to death in no time. That's why it hibernates; it's compelled to. Hibernation, in turn, requires it to lay on excessive fat, and this may be the reason for the low reproduction rate and also for the groundhog's comparatively short life. In the wild it is rare that a chuck lives to be five years old. The average span, I would say, is four years. Many don't emerge from their third winter.

The woodchuck comes from a race of fine home-builders, like the ground squirrel, prairie dog, pika. For instance, the home of that pert, harmless, delightful little scamp that the Indians called "Cheepmoinque" and we call chipmunk, is an elaborate affair consisting of a bedroom with a big, warm nest, a toilet room at the far end of a tunnel, a pantry well stocked with food, trapdoors too small for the murderous weasel or the thieving pine squirrel to squeeze through, and escape doors when the blacksnake comes marauding. Beyond any doubt the chipmunk's home has been a big factor in this little sassbox's survival and its prevalence today. So, how about the woodchuck's home—any help with our puzzle there?

Considering that the chuck is a fine digger, it is surprising to find, in excavating dens and exploring them with a probe, that the woodchuck burrow is not the well-engineered, well-kept animal home it is popularly supposed to be. It isn't at all elaborate, like the chipmunk's. It doesn't have good drainage or any anti-flooding device, like the prairie dog's little collar dike around the entrance. In brief, the chuck doesn't go to any more bother than it strictly has to, either in its engineering or its housekeeping.

A woodchuck seeking a den will always take over an empty burrow if it can find one. It digs a new den only if compelled to. Except for moles and perhaps the armadillo, it is surpassed in digging prowess only by its mortal enemy, the badger. I once experimented with a half-grown chuck and it tunneled through eight feet of firm clay in approximately an hour. I admit I spurred it on some by shooting off a .22 pistol at the entrance now and then, but even so that's fast work.

A new burrow consists at first of merely a single entrance and tunnel. Later on a side pocket is added, as a lay-up chamber, and after that a plunge hole. This is a vertical shaft, dug from the inside, the loose soil being pushed out the front door. Incidentally, a chuck doesn't kick the loose dirt out with its hind feet, like a dog or fox, but sort of bulldozes it out with its chest. Because the plunge hole lacks an apron of dirt and is hard to see, it's usually the hole that horses and cattle break their legs in.

Dens which have been occupied a long time often have many openings. A burrow with a dozen openings is common. My record number is nineteen. In a few instances the extra openings are chuck work; they're dug when the original tunnels and entrances get flooded or badly fouled up. But in the majority of cases the remodeling and additions are the work of foxes—red, gray and kit—which take over and enlarge chuck dens for the whelping period and then hand them back to the owners.

As for its home life and community activities, the woodchuck lives alone and likes it. Now and then two litter mates will occupy the same burrow till they're about three months old, and occasionally a mother chuck will permit one of her young to remain with her till it's about a third grown. But these are rare exceptions. Whereas other animals will bunch up sociably, the groundhog won't let a visitor even hang up his hat. If you cut a chuck off from its own burrow and drive it into another's den, you immediately hear a great to-do of whistling, teeth clicking and sibilant squealing, and pretty soon the intruder comes barging out, with maybe a bit of its tail chopped off. It's always the trespasser that gets ejected. A five-pound home owner will "bounce" a ten-pound intruder every time, and don't ask me how come.

Except in defending its home and at mating time, the chuck is not at all belligerent towards other chucks. But neither is it a social animal. All its habits and instincts are solitary. The right word is, I think, *indifferent*. It simply pays no attention to its neighbor, if it's got one. Two chucks will feed almost cheek to jowl without being aware the other exists, and repeatedly you'll see individuals pass each other on a chuck trail without so much as a sniff or a howd'y. The so-called marmot "colonies" of the northern Rockies aren't true colonies but merely accidental concentrations on some slope where the food and burrowing conditions are extra good.

Our last unexplored topic in this mystery of the woodchuck's abundance is the question of the chuck's mentality. This is a topic I'd just as soon avoid. Some years ago I published an "economic study" of the groundhog, and in the course of the article I stated that the mentality of the chuck was a bit low-grade as compared with other animals. Great day, what a spanking I got for that remark! Readers wrote in from all over, taking issue, defending the chuck as a most intelligent, sagacious creature, and saying that the only low-grade mentality involved was my own.

Here are a few simple observations which anyone can repeat and which indicate roughly the chuck's I.Q.:

In the spring a baited boxtrap in the back end of the garden will catch the same chuck several days hand run. Neither the skunk, rabbit or ol' pokey possum will go back and get caught in the same trap again and again.

If you're stalking a chuck in the open field and it sees you, just get a rock, tree or grazing cow between yourself and the chuck and you can walk right up on it. That trick won't fool the really bright boys, like the fox, wolf or bighorn.

If you walk downslope toward a chuck, you can get twice as close as by approaching uphill. During some phase of its development the woodchuck was exclusively a high-slope dweller, as the bighorn is today, so it watched mostly downhill because that's where its enemies came from. Thousands of years have passed since this habit was of any value; in fact, it's a liability now; but still the chuck keeps watching down the hill and pays little attention to the slope above.

One last example. The chuck has a formidable set of front teeth and if caught away from its hole it can defend itself effectively against the fox, small coyote and ordinary dog. By facing its enemy and daunting him with those ivory choppers, it usually succeeds in backing up to its den. All it needs to do is to keep on backing up, right down into its hole, and it would be safe. But no. The groundhog way of entering a burrow is head first, so it turns around and tries to plunge in. So its enemy grabs it by its unprotected hind quarters—and it's a dead chuck. Foxes are aware of this dumb groundhog habit. I have many times watched them follow half-grown chucks to the hole and seize them there. And Smoke too took advantage of this dumb habit. A superb woodchuck hunter, he was often borrowed by friends, where a chuck was ruining a garden, or by farmers with chuck-ridden fields; and he would actually herd a groundhog toward its hole so that he could dispatch it without getting bitten.

All this is not to say that the woodchuck is a complete nitwit. But definitely it's a cut below most other common animals, possibly because it eats itself dull and sluggish, and definitely there's nothing in its mentality to explain its great success and abundance.

One time I showed a wise old natural scientist a paper I had worked up on the different forms of animal play, which is an important activity with nearly all animals. In this paper I commented that woodchuck play is almost negligible; my notes covering twenty years of observation contained only half a dozen instances of it. When he read this the old naturalist remarked:

"Hmmph! The woodchuck is strictly business, isn't he?"

The remark didn't register with me just then. We got to talking about the woodchuck's abundance and my failure to crack the case of the abounding chuck, and after listening to my account the naturalist said:

"It seems to me that you've been looking for this 'hidden chuck asset' mostly on the physical level. Why don't you try looking deeper—into the woodchuck's nature, its *character*, so to speak? The different species of animals and birds have very different emotional make-ups, as you well know. Often a creature's dominant mental or emotional characteristic is a far sounder explanation of its fortunes than a sharper tooth or a longer wing feather."

There was a time, and not very long ago, when words like those would have been scientific heresy. They border on anthropomorphism, or ascribing human-like traits to the so-called lower creatures. They deny that animals are nothing but a complex of physical and chemical reactions, the product and the prisoner of environment. They assert that there is more to the mystery of life, even on the lower levels, than the materialistic ingredients of a physical and chemical nature. Yes, words like those would make Huxley turn over in his grave, and his successors would have shouted down the philosophy that animals have traits and emotions that are not unlike human traits and emotions, and that these play a large part, if not the dominant part, in the long-run fortunes of a species.

When I got back home that phrase "strictly business" somehow lingered in my mind. The more I pondered it, the more it seemed to open a door. Using it as a guide, I carefully went through all my woodchuck data and observational records. And what did I come up with? Why, a long list of groundhog "does not's." The chuck doesn't take dust baths, though the great majority of other animals and birds revel in these. It doesn't make a nest, except a poor, skimpy thing for newborn young and occasionally for hibernation. It doesn't fight, except as I've indicated. It doesn't associate with other chucks. It doesn't dig any more of a home than it has to. It doesn't—— But we can sum this all up by saying that it doesn't do a thing on earth it doesn't have to. Everything is stripped away down to the barest needs of mere existence.

Just take a look at the chuck's daily round. It comes out, feeds and at once goes back in again, into the dank safety of its den. There it sleeps till it's hungry, whereupon it comes out, feeds and trundles back in. Not one iota of energy or attention is "wasted" in play, neighborly association, family life or suchlike. Fully nine tenths of its life span, by actual figures, is spent underground, in the dark, silent security of its burrow. Most of the remaining one tenth is spent feeding.

The big point here is that by sacrificing most of the pleasanter values and activities of life the chuck cuts its exposure to enemies to the absolute minimum, eliminates any expenditure of energy not absolutely necessary, and puts the emphasis of its behavior pattern on avoiding risk.

Somebody once said that it isn't the bed cover on top of us that keeps us warm but what hangs down over the side. Don't tell that to the groundhog. He'd mutter "Nonsense!" and go on munching clover. As far as efficiency is concerned, efficiency in living safe and keeping alive amid the dangers of an open-field habitat, I know of no comparable animal that can equal it. Its low reproduction rate, its slowness of foot, its unimpressive I.Q., its other serious handicaps—all these are outweighed by this dominating characteristic of playing it safe.

In view of the chuck's big increase and tremendous numbers today, we have to admit that this characteristic has proved uniquely successful. The wolf has nearly vanished in the United States, the wily catamount is now confined to a few rugged regions, the passenger pigeon myriads are no more, but the obscure, heavy-footed chuck abounds everywhere, and often, sitting bolt upright on a sunny hillside, it's the only wild creature of any size that we see for miles and miles.

I fervently hope that the chuck remains abundant. His enormous appetite and his destructiveness to pastures and field crops have recently drawn attention to him as a costly pest, and undoubtedly he is in for a bad time of it up ahead, with dairymen, orchardists and farmers generally. But in wild land, where he does no damage, he can and should be protected. Without his whistle, his dumpy figure standing beside his door, his periscope eye looking at you from a nearby hole, the outdoors wouldn't be the same.

But nevertheless I believe we feel that the chuck's success has been purchased at a pretty fearful price. And I'm sure that the chipmunk and the bob-o-link, the otter, the cheery cardinal and all the other creatures that prefer to live perilously would agree with us and would say that the woodchuck can keep his dull safety—they'll take the sunshine and winds, the dangers and also the delights, of the outdoors and the open sky.

Wild Salads

"DOWN north" in sub-Arctic Canada, where the permafrost makes truck gardening impossible and air freightage is costly, people sometimes get on queer hankers for green stuff. Take the fellows that time at the prospecting camp in the Liard Rockies. When ex-Mounty Dave Adams and myself put down there one evening in that old Bellanca Pacemaker, bringing in their mail and supplies, but *no lettuce*, they were fit to be tied.

A proving-up crew of ten or eleven men, they had been back in there over a month, working a dozen hours a day and eating mostly meat, beans and suchlike, and they were hungry as spring bears for something in the green-salad line. They had got word out and ordered four crates of head lettuce from Edmonton, but Adams and I hadn't known about this, so their precious lettuce, costing about two hundred dollars in air freight, sat rotting in a plane-pier shed over on Great Slave.

As soon as he sized up their trouble, Adams got busy and in just a few minutes he conjured up a salad for them. It was not only the biggest salad I ever saw put on a table but was tastier and better than could be bought most places at any price.

This wasn't the first time I had seen this green-stuff hunger down there in the Territories. During the long winter back in the Barrens, trappers would eat reindeer moss, bogberries, willow buds or the tart, acidy contents of caribou stomach, to satisfy their want for something besides meat and quick bread. When they came out to the Mackenzie posts in the spring, the first thing they would do was to wireless Edmonton for a crate of lettuce or other greens, though the cost might run as high as seventy-five dollars a crate.

What Adams did was to take a potato sack and start up along a little stream toward a falls pool, gathering this and that—plantain, cress, a few spriggles of savory herbs. When he came back, he fixed up a simple, tasty dressing for his stuff, and those men sat down to a small washtub full of an appetizing salad that their tired head lettuce couldn't have touched for freshness and food value.

"Imagine it," Adams said to me later. "Wanting green stuff all that bad, and they had enough of it all around them to feed a young army."

A person doesn't have to be a lettuce-hungry hardrocker "down north" to profit from knowing about the fine wild greens that are available nearly everywhere. Anybody at all who enjoys the outdoors ought to know three or four wild-salad plants. Hunters, fishermen and others who go camping can save themselves the trouble of carrying in green stuff, which is bulky and also deteriorates badly, and there is nothing like a fresh, crisp salad to lighten up the usual heavy camp meal of meat and fish. Besides this, there is a certain deep satisfaction in getting our food afield, out of Nature's own garden.

There are many different wild-salad plants and a person trying to learn them all would get bogged down in botany. If you would like to gather wild greens, either at home or on camping trips, you need to know only a few kinds, at least to begin with, and certainly those kinds should be plants that are common, abundant and widely distributed. If you know them by sight already, so much the better. After learning how to gather and use them, you can easily add other plants to your list, one by one.

I myself know perhaps a couple of dozen wild greens but of these I gather only eight or nine kinds. As a matter of fact, I find that I depend mostly on only four, and those four I am going to emphasize here. They are my mainstays, the ones I gather regularly, and they are found everywhere, north and south, two of them north to the Arctic Circle. Besides being always available on camping trips or knocking around in Canada, they keep me in greens for at least ten months of the year; greens of a freshness and high quality that can't be bought, as I will explain later.

To mention again that "down north" hankering for green stuff, the nutrition experts tell us that this hunger isn't imaginary but is based on real body needs and in a healthy person can become clamorous, as with those fellows at the Liard camp. Leafy greens contain vitamin A, plus several valuable B's, plus the important "trace minerals," and in addition they supply certain enzymes and other food elements obtainable from no other source. Modern clinical tests which reveal nutritional deficiencies show that a surprising percentage of people have a low-grade "hidden hunger" for green stuff and suffer mild to serious ailments because of this lack.

Well, that's one deficiency I don't have and don't expect to get, and if you'll come along with me I'll show you what I mean. . . .

Ten minutes' walk from my back door there is a spring-fed pool, maybe thirty feet across, at the foot of a wooded slope. With its clear, cold water and bright-green vegetation, it's a very pretty spot, especially when snow covers the ground and the verdancy of the pool contrasts with the bare, gaunt trees. But that's not the point. In that pool there are three different watercresses which I can gather most of the winter, even when the surface is frozen over and I have to break the ice.

We may as well tackle right here that vexing question of the various kinds of watercress. A person who isn't a botanist can spin himself dizzy trying to make precise identifications of the many varieties and species. I just don't try, except when I run onto something extra good and want to know what it is. Some of the cresses we find outdoors are native American species, and their range is all over the United States and Canada, to Alaska and the Mackenzie country. Others, especially in the eastern states and provinces, are imports or escapes. That is, they were brought over from Britain or the Continent as cultivated strains and then "escaped" to the wild. To confuse the picture still further, there seems to be a certain amount of hybridizing going on among the members of this group.

So if you can't identify your plant down to a taxonomist's eyelash, don't worry. If it's watercress, it's good.

Typically watercress is a plant of small to medium size, seldom over a foot high, and it's a hydrophyte or "water lover." Sometimes you find it growing entirely under water, sometimes partly in and partly out, sometimes on land but in very wet soil. It has a whitish, succulent root, many hair roots, and rootlet nodules up and down the stem. Its flower, in spring and summer, has four petals, arranged in the form of a cross, whence the family name of Cruciferae. But the most easily identifiable feature of this group is the rosette of leaves at the top of the plant. Take a look at some cultivated cress in your grocery store and you won't fail to recognize this crown rosette when you see it afield.

Some watercresses are quite peppery. Those with too much bite can be mixed with some combiner, like lamb's-quarters, plantain or head lettuce. Other varieties are almost bland, a few entirely bland. These can be eaten just by themselves, with a bit of dressing.

Let me tell you something about those watercress roots. *Eat 'em.* They're not only tender and tasty but are swarming with enzymes and trace minerals.

Once you start looking for it you'll find watercress nearly everywhere outdoors that the habitat is at all suitable—in streams, ponds, marshland, wet meadows, spring pools—and the best varieties are available throughout the winter, unless the water freezes all the way to the bottom. It grows in thick mats and islands and very abundantly; patches covering a quarter acre are not uncommon. It occurs all over the United States and most of Canada, in settled country and wild, in highland and lowland—few indeed are the places where you can't find it readily.

In a rugged and severe section of the Peace River country I once encountered an abundant cress which was extra delicious but had features that puzzled me no end. I felt sure I had a new species and sent specimens to Ottawa. They wrote back saying this cress had been known for maybe a thousand years and probably had been brought to that region by some Hudson Bay person. Well, it was a mighty good one anyhow, and it kept our camp meals from being a succession of fish and canned stuff.

To illustrate cress abundance, there must be two dozen places within hiking distance of my home where I could gather watercress. But that pool I mentioned grows two species so good that I seldom go elsewhere. Its third species is too peppery for me. In gathering cress, I pull it up carefully, roots and all, using an old bent table fork tied to a stick. I take home enough each time for half a dozen meals. If footed in water, either in the icebox or in a large flat container in the basement, it will keep fine for about ten days and so will be absolutely fresh when you eat it.

This matter of freshness is really vital with leafy greens, and it's one big reason why the greens you gather outdoors and eat at once are incomparably higher in food values than the grocery store item. You know the old saying about fish—"from hook to kettle." Well, you can double that for leafy greens. They lose as much as thirty per cent of their value if not eaten within an hour of picking, and some of the more fragile properties are entirely lost in a couple of hours. Considering that store greens are usually many hours old, or even days, you can see that a salad of wild greens has a food value that can't be bought at any price.

When I prepare watercress myself, I merely cut it up, roots and all, and use a salad dressing of my own making. This dressing is about as simple as you can get them, but it tastes good, you can whip up a batch in two minutes, it lasts indefinitely, goes well with almost any greens, and it isn't all hopped up with strong spices and flavorings. The ingredients are: (1) Malt vinegar (or tarragon, if you wish), diluted half and half with water; (2) brown sugar; (3) a sprinkle of salt; (4) a sparing amount of clear, light salad oil or its equivalent. You proportion the sugar and vinegar to fit your individual taste.

On camping trips I always make up a supply of this dressing and take it along, to save lugging different items, and I suggest you do the same. In that old Bellanca down in the Mackenzie country, where meals were a bit uncertain—except that they would be fish and meat, or meat and fish—we usually had a padded jug of this dressing in the fuselage cubby. When I knock off work in the late afternoon and go out for a breath of country air, I carry a small, wide-necked jar of it in my tote bag and often eat some extra-fine greens on the spot.

When I mentioned plantain previously, you may have thought, "What—*that weed?*" That's how it's commonly regarded, I know—a lowly weed, a lawn and garden pest. Few people are aware that it's an edible plant, which the pioneers used extensively and which still is eaten quite a deal in certain sections, like the Ozarks. When I was a boy I ate lots of plantain greens.

Some years ago I saw a food properties analysis of plantain which placed it near the top of all the greens studied. Later, in the course of observing woodchuck feeding habits, I noticed that the chuck, who surely knows his way around among green things because he eats three to four pounds of them every day, chooses plantain above every other food except red-clover blossoms. On many an occasion outdoors, from Texas to Hudson Bay, I've been able to have a fresh, fine salad of plantain when other salad plants were scarce or absent. In brief, I regard it very highly among wild greens, as a stand-by, an old dependable and a mighty nutritious dish.

By all means try it yourself. Give it a fair trial, along the lines suggested below, and see what you think.

The plantains have a very wide distribution. They occur

on seashore and mountain, in our South and all the way to the Arctic, in semi-desert and in semi-swamp; and their forms differ considerably in these varying habitats. In the Mackenzie Delta region the dwarfed Arctic species, *Plantago borealis*, grows profusely, and on the granite swells of the eastern Great Slave it is one of the half dozen most common plants.

All the plantains have strongly ribbed leaves; hence the vernacular names of ribwort, rib grass, etc. Of the ten to twenty kinds of plantains (the number depending on whether the botanist is a "splitter" or a "lumper") none are noxious or harmful. Some, however, have tough or woolly leaves, tough cords in the veins or other undesirable features. These can merely be discarded or avoided. The best varieties, it seems to me, are those smaller ones with smooth, rather shiny leaves of a roundish or broad-ovate form, rather than long and narrow leaves. But I'm not certain about even this rule, because one of the best plantains I ever ate, a kind I found along the railroad about a hundred miles from Churchill, had a leaf that was decidedly lanceolate.

I suppose some people would object to plantain on the grounds of toughness. Well, it isn't as tender as lush-grown lettuce, but if you chop it up fine with scissors it's tender enough. Being very bland, or without much taste except that of chlorophyll green, plantain does best when combined with some plant like peppery cress, or garnished with one of the savory herbs, which I'll get around to presently, or used with some dressing that supplies a tang and a bite.

One big talking point for plantain is that it is available everywhere and usually abundant enough that you can gather a mess in a few minutes. Another recommendation is that it keeps coming throughout the summer, the young, tender plants being mixed in with the older ones but readily discernible. Also, it is easier than most greens to wash and prepare.

But the main point about *Plantago* is that in food value it outranks any grocery-store greens several times over and tops most of the wild greens. The reason for this is interesting and instructive and can be stated in two words: it is *slow growing*. For instance, a plantain of the common broad-leaf kind will take several weeks attaining a length of four or five inches, whereas some lush, cultivated greens will attain three times that length and half a dozen times that weight. There is a general nutritional law to the effect that, other things being equal, the slow-growing food item, whether it be greens, vegetable, fruit or even meat, has a higher nutritional value than the forced or quick-grown item.

According to extensive studies, the so-called "tropic lethargy" is due mostly to a deficiency of vitamins and other food elements in tropic-grown foods, and this deficiency in turn is due to the fact that things grow quickly in the tropics. But things can be made to grow quickly in the temperate latitudes too, under forced cultivation, and these quickie items can be just as deficient as the tropic items.

When clinical tests reveal a deficiency of the food elements supplied by leafy greens, the person involved will often insist that he does eat these greens regularly and in sufficient quantity. In those cases the explanation is that the greens are ruined by overcooking or else were of poor quality to begin with. That is, they were tired and stale, or were quick grown, or both. Our humble friend *Plantago* takes its time, grows slowly, and when you gather it fresh it is chock full of the food values that leafy greens ought to have but so often don't.

In southeastern Europe, way back in the Old Stone Age, the cave man discovered that a certain wild plant went well with his roast reindeer and wild pony. He drew pictures of it on his cave walls. When he finally learned to sow and cultivate, it was one of the first plants he raised. Later, as the millenia passed, he bred this plant and its immediate kin into a large number of pot-herbs. The various kinds of spinach and beets and many other food plants known locally in eastern Europe and Asia are all derived from this source.

If you will go out and look around in your garden, or any weed patch, fallow field or open place around your camp site, you'll find plenty of that original wild plant. It ranges up to two feet in height, has leaves somewhat resembling a goose track in shape, and has a silver-dust effect on the under side of the leaves and around the petioles or leaf stems.

Botanists call this plant *Chenopodium album*. Common names are goosefoot, lamb's-quarters, pigweed and wild spinach. I wouldn't know why it's called pigweed unless it's because pigs, along with other creatures who know a good thing when they see it, go for *C. album* in a big way.

There are many native American plants of the goosefoot family, but except for a couple, like Mexican Tea, they have not been investigated, as they certainly should be. I have no doubt that some of them are excellent greens. But here we will talk only about the specific plant *C. album*, or lamb's-quarters. Although an import, it is very common and abundant through the East, lower Canada and west to the Mississippi, and is rapidly spreading elsewhere.

Some people seem to believe that lamb's-quarters is a springtime greens only. On the contrary, it is best in early summer and can be eaten till fall. The only difference is that in spring the whole plant can be eaten, whereas in late summer the stems may be a bit on the tough side and it's best to use only the leaves.

Like any other greens, lamb's-quarters delivers its maximum food value if eaten uncooked. Those who like a more pronounced taste can combine it with another greens or garnish it with a savory herb.

I do admit that cooked lamb's-quarters, especially in midsummer, when the greens won't "mush up" so much, is quite delicious. But when we do cook it we ought to do this right. Oh, the murders that are committed on leafy greens with pot and kettle! They ought to be cooked as little as possible, with as little water as possible, and the pot liquor, which contains most of those invaluable trace minerals and a good deal of the water-soluble vitamins, should be saved and used. But many a cookbook tells you to parboil greens for several minutes, throw the liquid away and then boil some more. That's culinary murder.

The procedure which all the Home Ec and nutrition experts agree on is this: put your water on the stove, using as little as possible, and salt lightly; bring to a boil and then put in your greens, and cook only until they are well wilted and have not yet lost all their natural green color. This usually means from one to three minutes.

With lamb's-quarters I vary this procedure a little. I dice several strips of bacon and fry till crisp. Then I dump the bacon and grease into boiling water, put in the greens and cook these for two minutes. The dish can be garnished with a dab of butter and a jigger of tarragon vinegar. The pot liquor can be fancied up the same way. Try cooking lamb's-quarters like this, and you'll say you've struck something good.

There's a story about a big game hunter in Alaska who saw a sign nailed to a tree back in the brush and asked his guide what it said. "Why that," the guide informed him, "is the city limits of Los Angeles." I don't suppose that this hunter was more surprised than I was once, tooting across the Big Portage on the Slave, when I ran onto a big expanse of our old friend dandelion, growing bravely all over a sandy ridge, along with dwarf strawberries and dwarf lupine.

In the matter of extending its limits, dandelion (*dens leonis*, or lion's tooth) goes even Los Angeles one better. Originally a plant of the warm Mediterranean lands, it extended its range all over Europe, then jumped the Atlantic and now grows everywhere from Florida to the sub-Arctic.

An ancient name for dandelion in northern Europe was "scurvy plant," in reference to its worth in warding off or curing scurvy. It was always the first greens available in the spring, after a long winter of foods that lacked the leafy-green elements. Over here it likewise was and is the first fresh greens. It appears with the peeper frogs and kill-deers, and in my book the first dish of dandelions is an event, like the first morel mushrooms, the first mess of yellow perch caught through the ice and that first bowl of wild strawberries.

I just don't know why people keep saying that dandelions are good only in the spring. Great day, the midsummer crop of young plants is much better than the spring crop. You can gather dandelions from March to November, young plants or old ones. I prefer them all uncooked. You may like the older plants cooked a bit.

A warm salad dressing goes fine with dandelions, so I'll give you one here, an old-fashioned recipe which is easy to fix and can be used with any leafy-green salad:

Gather and wash enough dandelions to make a quart, moderately firm packing. Fry ⅕ lb. bacon till crisp. Beat up an egg, add ¼ cup sugar, ¼ cup water, ¼ cup vinegar. Pour this in with the bacon and stir till the dressing thickens, then pour it over the dandelions. If you want to, garnish with slices of hard-boiled egg. This makes enough to serve three people generously.

Let me tell you about a dandelion dish which isn't greens exactly but is mighty fine just the same. Gather a pan of dandelion blossoms, wash in cold water, dip lightly in egg batter, and fry them for two or three minutes in moderately hot grease. If you haven't eaten this dish, try it once on my say-so. After that, you won't need anybody's say-so.

Well, that's the Big Four among wild greens—plantain, lamb's-quarter, dandelion and watercress. They are abundant, grow nearly everywhere, are known already or easily identifiable, are very wholesome and high in food values. Without going outside of them you can have a fine, wild-greens salad every day for at least ten months out of the year. But in case you want to add some other plants to your list, here are a few suggestions:

Wild chicory (*Cichorium intybus*) makes a good green, either raw or cooked, if you get it before the familiar blue flowers appear. In some regions this plant is called "succory." In the Maritimes and Newfoundland it's called "blue sailors." If it's a pest in your garden, keep it down by eating it.

Purslane (*Portulaca oleracea*) is abundant in most of the states except the northern tier. This is one of the few greens that I like best cooked.

Horse-radish, an escape plant, is found quite widely now in the wild. The tender tops are wholesome and good in spring. Later they develop too much bite.

Although several of the docks are widely used as greens, I myself don't gather them and I don't advise anybody to except the expert botanist. There is a great deal of confusion in the common usage of the word "dock." In some sections almost any large, broad-leafed plant is called a dock. I have actually heard this name applied to Jimson weed. Even among the true docks some species are not entirely wholesome, and it's hard for the amateur to distinguish between the good and the bad. There's no point to eating any questionable plant when we have so many fine, dependable greens all around.

Young poke shoots, which you hear so much about and which is the celebrated "poke sallit" of the southern hill regions, is another greens that should be approached with caution. If gathered when the shoots are only a few inches high and cooked properly, they are admittedly good. But young raspberry shoots are just as good and they're safe, whereas poke shoots become unwholesome when they get over a foot high, because of an alkaloid substance. Also, a person has to be careful not to get any part whatever of the root with the shoots. The root is bitter and mildly poisonous.

None of the mosses, at least that I know about, make acceptable food, except perhaps "reindeer moss." When cooked, this becomes a gelatinous mass that will stave off hunger but doesn't have much food value.

Some of the ferns are said to make good greens. The only one I have eaten is the fiddle fern (or fiddle-head fern). This should be gathered early in the spring, before the young curls unfold, the curls being used. They should be cooked. But at this stage ferns are hard to distinguish and some ferns are not wholesome. For instance, the male fern or sweet brake contains a substance which is a vermifuge.

All over the southern states the cultivated varieties of spinach and mustard have escaped and become widely established in the wild. These volunteer plants are much better, being slower growing, than the greens under cultivation. In fact, this volunteer mustard is the finest of all pot-herbs, bar none. It has a little too much bite to eat raw, unless mixed with some bland greens, or a couple of leaves in a bread and butter sandwich. But when cooked right, with a little salt pork, and a dash of vinegar to season it, there's no pot-herb that can match it or even come close. . . .

The so-called "savory herbs" which I have mentioned are not greens at all and should not be thought of as such. They are flavoring ingredients. The thing to remember about them is that they should not be eaten in quantity.

This is because they contain some "essential oil," such as oil of peppermint, oil of sage, oil of pepper, which can cause a stomach upset or bowel irritation if very much is eaten.

But used in moderation, as garnish or flavoring agent, they can step up a dish of greens, of meat or fish or potatoes, or a drink, or a soup or stew most pleasantly.

Wild mint, grated or chopped fine, adds a lot to any potato dish, including camp fries. Pepper grass or shepherd's-purse adds piquancy to a bland salad, like plantain. And try wrapping your fish or meat in wild grape leaves sometime.

The savory herbs most commonly met with outdoors are wild parsley, wild thyme, wild basil, the several mints, pepper grass, sweet anise or wild licorice and wild garlic.

This last, wild garlic, is easily the best of all the savory herbs, in my book. I wouldn't get caught dead up an alley eating store garlic, but the wild article, a dainty little plant like a diminutive onion, is something entirely different. It grows profusely everywhere and can be gathered all the year. The bulb seldom gets larger than the eraser on your lead pencil, and is not so strong but that it can be eaten alone, with salt and bread. The straw-slender, onionlike top can be chopped up as a garnish. On many a winter day I've gone over to that pool I mentioned and got a bunch of that bright-green, bland watercress, and dug up five or six wild garlic plants on the way home, and mixed the two into a salad, with the simple salad dressing I told you about, and had myself a dish you couldn't buy for the proverbial love or money.

'Seng Hunter

SOMEBODY had shadowed me up the lonely, old-beech hollow, and had slipped up unseen to easy gun distance. It made the back of my neck feel crawly, like ants running up and down, to have an unknown individual watching me like that. For all I knew, he was studying me over a rifle barrel and waiting for a good heart shot.

This was one of those places in the deep Ozarks where it isn't good policy for a stranger to go drifting around in the woods. It's true that most of those stories you hear or read in regard to "furriners" getting potted on sight are a plain libel on those hill people, who average as kind and friendly as any people I know of. If you can show business, honest and regular business, the only copperheads you meet are the sort that crawl on their bellies. But back-county folk mostly have to look out for themselves, and if a suspicious character insists on poking or molesting around, he does run a risk of getting "snake-bit." And I was not only a stranger thereabouts but a city person to boot.

Down the hollow from me there was a tangle of laurel,

mossy boulders and stately old beeches, and I knew that my silent-footed customer was somewhere in that tangle. But I couldn't locate him exactly. Whoever he could be, he was a honey of a woodsman. So far I hadn't heard the slightest rustle or caught even a flit-glimpse of him.

Trying to act unconcerned, I kept on with my business, which was digging out a small spread of ginseng beside the little stream. But you can bet I was doing some fast thinking. A rifle would have felt mighty fortifying just then. If I'd had one, I would have ducked behind the nearest boulder and taken this fellow on at a little game of hide-and-seek. As a born-and-bred hillikin myself, with a wild-colt background of bush-loping, trapping and root hunting, I wasn't any slouch at taking care of myself in the woods, excusing a little city rustiness.

But I didn't have a rifle, or even a pocket gun, or anything except a digging stick. The woods up the hollow were so open that I wouldn't have stood any chance if I'd made a break. Besides, the hollow was fenced in by a high rimrock, all the way around.

The thing to do—and I made myself do it—was to keep on digging 'seng and hope that my friend in the laurel would be decent about things; decent enough to ask questions first.

It was the midday lull; the birds had stopped feeding, the fox squirrels had stopped cutting, and the hollow was dead quiet except for the tinkle of its little stream. Miles away across the hills and sedge uplands I faintly heard the noon whistle of the saw-yards at the small Ozark town where I was stopping for four days, during a vacation trip from my home over in New York.

A late August heat wave was frying the whole Midwest. Chicago, St. Louis, Willow Springs and the hill town had been sticky and sweltering. But even at high hot noon the hollow was cool and dim. Now and then you still hear the Smoky (Indian) name for those rimrocked hollows—*koni-konishas*. Just an ordinary hollow would be a *konisha;* but one that's so deep and heavily timbered that it holds a linger of twilight at midday, so quiet that it's like a Sunday hush, and so moist and rich that the moss covers all the ground and boulders and runs part-way up the hoary old beech trunks—that extra-special, extra-wild, churchlike hollow is a *koni-konisha.*

A while passed and nothing happened. It began to look as though the two-legged shadow in those laurels did intend to ask questions first. But I couldn't be sure. Willynilly my imagination kept running on a pretty dreadful little business I'd once met with in a north Georgia woods —a man sitting in a clump of willow-stump sprouts, so natural-like that I all but spoke to him before seeing that he was a couple of days dead, with a bullet hole in the nape of his skull. Evidently somebody had been stalking him and he had tried to hide in the screen of sprouts. I didn't want to sit and wait, as that poor cuss had done, for somebody to come along and think I looked natural-like.

Pretty soon I saw a red fox jump up on a boulder in the

laurel clump, about thirty yards away. I wondered for a second if this could be the creature which had trailed me up the hollow, touching off those alarm calls of the vireos and titmice. But no, the intruder was a human. He was hidden, a few steps back of the fox. The way I knew was that a hummingbird was making angry little power-dives at him.

It figured that the fox was a tame thing belonging to the man. So much time had passed by now that I felt reasonably hopeful I would be given a chance to talk, after the fellow got through studying me. But even so I didn't feel I would be off the hook. I couldn't show any regular and honest business in there. To a suspicious stranger my story, true or not, just didn't hold water. A New Yorker, all alone in an Ozark *koni-konisha* five miles from the nearest sidewalk, digging up a root dollar or so that I didn't need—it was one of those freaky situations that make sense only to yourself. It happened this way:

With a few days free from university lecturing and a long research job, I had whipped out to the Ozarks to freshen up old-time acquaintanceships and breathe the hills again. A rigid timetable called for covering several counties fast, giving each one a lick and a promise. But on my very first morning in the hills, I'd taken a little walk before breakfast, just into the woods at the edge of town, and there I'd run onto some ginseng and yellow puccoon. The old 'seng-hunting fever came back like a flash flood, and my fine plans all dropped out of mind. Back in town I picked up some grub, got an ironshod digging stick at the blacksmith's, and shot the whole day—and all the rest of my vacation—roaming the near hills and hollows for 'seng.

The tame fox set me to thinking that the man might be a 'seng hunter. Not the pennyroyal farmer or town loafer who digs a little on the side, but the genuine article. I'd met a few of these woods hermits. They live wholly outdoors in the hills, all year, drifting north up across the Ozarks in summer and back to southern Arkansas in winter. Occasionally they slip into some hill town to sell their roots and buy a few elementaries like salt, matches, painkiller and maybe a new knife or leather pants. Now and then one of them will stay long enough to soak up some sociability, at a dance or a church meeting, but mostly they shy off from associating with people.

I surely hoped that my friend in the laurels was a genuine 'seng hunter. Here and there I'd met half a dozen of them, and they'd all been safe and decent individuals. I'd never seen or heard of one toting a gun or frog-sticker. And they never quarrel about territory, digging rights or suchlike. Their attitude, as nearly as I can state it, is that the hills belong to the Lord and no man can claim things like 'seng, wild fruit, wild creatures or anything he doesn't plant or tend.

It was a good half hour, and a mighty long half hour, before the man in the laurel allowed me to have a look at him. He had moved a little up the hillside, in deep brush, and was poking around with his stick, to make out he was just digging some roots. By this time I knew for certain he was a regular 'seng hunter. No other person would have studied me that long or been so cautious about disclosing himself. Usually all you ever see of a 'seng hunter is a glimpse of the fellow, off in the woods somewhere, watching you a minute or so and then fading. Sometimes you don't even see that much.

It finally became clear that this 'seng hunter had some special business with me. That was why he'd trailed me and was giving me such a long looking-over. I was figuring him now as entirely safe, but what under the sun he wanted was a first-rate puzzle.

I knew better than to call out or try to rush acquaintance. Any loud or abrupt move, and a timid 'seng hunter might flush like a deer and wind up halfway across two counties. I merely nodded in his direction, like a casual "How-do, friend," and kept on minding my business.

After digging the rest of the patch, I finished replanting the seedlings I'd uprooted, and also I bedded in the seeds from the ripe red pods, so that whoever came drifting up that mossy *koni-konisha*, in five, six years would find him a 'seng patch as good as I'd found. I saw the fellow move out in plainer view and watch me replanting, and when I looked straight at him he didn't ease out of sight. Whatever he wanted, he seemed to believe I might fit the bill.

While the man started edging down toward me, I washed my roots and spread them on a rock to drain. The roots would dry out to maybe a quarter pound, about three dollars' worth. It set me to remembering my hillikin-colt days and what fine money those 'seng dollars had been. They were big as wagon wheels. But that was hardly half the story. The main thing, they were sweet dollars. You dug them out of the woods loam, back in the free wild hills, to the low tune of a waterfall and a chipmunk sassing you; and they were the sweetest dollars a person ever earned. And if you were good, if you had a natural eye for spotting the peculiar green of the 'seng leaf among the snakeroot, grape fern and other woods-floor plants, you could make lots better wages than hacking ties or husking corn at the big-valley farms. I hit one single patch once that dug out eighty-some dollars' worth. The granddaddy plants, always uphill from the seedlings and two-prongs, had reached from the stream clear up to the rimrock.

As the 'seng hunter edged up closer and closer, I began talking around casually and pretty soon he began putting in some talk. The fox was sticking tight against his legs and eying me timidly. They are usually very much a one-man dog, pathetically afraid of all humans except the one that breathed on its nose as a pup. Their chief use is for companionship, against the day-in and day-out loneliness. They work out better than a dog for a 'seng hunter; they can pick off rabbits for him on the fly, rustle their own grub, and they don't go yelping around through the quiet woods or chasing the town cats.

The 'seng hunter, a lean, medium-tall fellow of about

thirty, had on mahogany leather pants, neat lace-pacs and a buckskin shirt. His face was weathered as dark as a Smoky's, and he had that faint smoky odor of many campfires. All the man's possessions were what he wore and carried—his digging stick, a little blanket roll, a somewhat larger roll of cookery items. I envied him his silent feet and his lithe, catamount gracefulness. But it seemed a pity for a fine, youngish fellow like him to be so uneasy toward another man, toward all humans in fact. It made for painfulness and it was thoroughly unnecessary. It all sprang from nothing more than a notion in his brain.

He went for cigarettes and we smoked a couple apiece while we talked around, mostly about the woods. Although he was too polite to pry, I could see he was puzzled no end at me—an individual who had a hillikin tongue but wore the togs of a city dude; who was digging 'seng in the woods that day and flying back to New York the next. So I told him about the early times and how I liked to get back when I could and get a snootful of the hills.

He understood this surprisingly well. "Yuh," he said, "I knowed it was someway liken that with you." He nodded at the 'seng patch. "When I seen you a-seeding that back, 'stead of leaving it all rooted up and ruint the way some hawgish folks do, I purely knowed you warn't borned no curbstone Johnny."

This told me why I'd passed muster with him, but it didn't give any hint what he wanted of me.

After a little spell, when he had got free and easy

enough, I opened my lunch creel. You should have seen his eyes bug out when I poked a hole in the bottom of a cold can, then opened the can and poured him a cup of hot coffee. To anybody who might have considered him backwoods he would have made out that he knew all about this city-dude wrinkle, but I was handling him careful, and in his grave way he remarked, "Now ain't that a dido proper!" And when I forked him some hot beans from a second can, he shook his head unbelievingly. "By lords and by jedus, 'tis the beat of anything I ever seen, by a mile and a toad hop!"

We ate and smoked and talked. Once the ice is broken, a 'seng hunter likes to talk. It may seem strange but in reality they're pitifully hungry for human company. If that seems contradictory to the way they avoid people—well, we've all got contradictions like that. If we keep them in hand, it's all right; in fact it's a healthy situation, like the Democrats and Republicans always fighting each other. It makes them both toe the line. But when a contradiction gets out of hand, it can do damage, and that's the trouble with 'seng hunters.

When they go into a town or meet up with somebody, they can't tolerate being stared at, like some odd specimen, and especially getting laughed at. In all likelihood 'seng hunters are individuals who were a little queer and sensitive to begin with, and their living alone makes them queerer still. Nine times out of ten, when they show up in a town the girls titter at them and the fellows start lobbing jokes back and forth, not really meaning anything bad. But after a few years of that, you've got a human being who won't even approach you in the woods unless he's studied your angles for a while and feels you're all right.

My skittish friend—his name was Marlen—seemed to me exceptionally sensitive, and he had no reason on earth for it. He was as hard and handsome as a young hickory, and he had a reasonably good mind. Put him into a suit of store clothes, currycomb him a little and teach him some fiddle-footing, and he could have walked off with any Tess or Judy at the dance. His slow, dignified talk was laced with the earthy pioneerisms of a full century ago. You could shut your eyes and almost imagine yourself listening to Boone or Crockett or young Abe.

We must have talked for an hour, and still I hadn't any idea what Marlen wanted. He himself, in spite of his liking human company, got up and broke off the talk. His reason was downright considerate.

"Bein's as this evening"—he meant afternoon—"is the onliest time you've got left to your holiday, I figger you'd ruther not waste it chinchabbering with me thisaway. So me and Rusty here, we'll put on our feet and git along, and you kin work the balance of this holler." He picked up the discarded sandwich sack and put it into his poke. "Come sundown, mebbe me and Rusty will be crossing you ag'in, down yon by the valley road."

I hunted on up to the head of the hollow, where the little stream tumbled down from the hundred-foot rimrock.

After taking a dip in the pool there and sitting myself dry on a sunny rock, I started back down the *koni-konisha*, to meet Marlen and then get back to town and close out my stay in the hills.

I kept thinking it was a pity that the 'seng hunters mix so little with the rest of us. They never were more than a handful, and according to what I keep hearing they are dwindling out pretty fast. They have something to give other people: an example of living simple, living next to the earth. But it goes to waste with them, because they're human-shy. It was particularly sad to see a young fellow like Marlen getting farther and farther lost on that one-way trail.

The evening shadows came early in the deep, rocky *koni-konisha*. When I got down to the mouth of the hollow and looked back, the *koni-konisha* was filling with owl dusk and the whippoorwills were starting up, though it was still good light in the valley.

Marlen was waiting for me at a little drogue (grove) of second-growth oak a few rods from the valley road. To pay me back for the lunch, I guess, he had got a meal ready—young fried rabbit, oystershell mushrooms, some belated roast-ears he had probably swiped, some watercress mixed with tart woods sorrel, and a pot of ruby sassafras tea.

"Thought mebbe you'd care to squat and eat with me and Rusty," he invited.

"Damn all, I can't, Marlen," I said. The town taxi which

was to pick me up was already a bit overdue. Why I didn't make the taxi wait, why I didn't stay for that supper instead of rushing back to the dusty town, I really don't know.

Marlen was disappointed. He probably half believed I was brushing him off.

He listened down valley and said, before I could hear anything, "The machine is a-coming for you." He handed me a small poke of dry 'seng roots, and a piece of the paper sack, with some writing on it. "They's a little favor, there in town—'twon't take you more'n a minute or so——"

"Why sure, Marlen," I said. This was it—the thing he'd been hanging around for, half a day. I looked at the piece of sack. He had whittled a red ocher pebble to a point and printed out a small list of elementaries.

"If you kindly so," he said, "you mighten hand this list to Sam Burgoon, at his store, and give him this poke of 'seng to pay for the things. Ask him to putten 'em in a gunny sack and hang the sack outside his back door, and I'll be picking it up some time in the night."

In spite of the fact that I'd known Marlen was an extrashy 'seng hunter, his little request took me by surprise like getting hit by a hornet. A human being who wouldn't go into town except by night, when nobody would see him— that was a little the worst case I'd ever known.

Marlen noticed my surprise. Not wanting me to believe he was queer, he explained rather lamely: "It's a-cause of Rusty here; the town dogs persecute him so. I know 'xactly how he feels. It purely cuddles his blood to have them town dogs a-barking around and eying him through the picket fences and taking nips at him, jest a-cause he's a woods thing."

I chewed it all over for a minute. The taxi came dusting around a bend, stopped on the valley road and started honking. I shook hands with Marlen and promised to do his errand at the Burgoon store. Then I said, hoping it might be like one of the seeds I'd planted that day:

"Look, Marlen—you tell Rusty not to mind the town dogs so much. They bark around and eye him, I know, but if Rusty would just perk his tail up in the air and go trotting down the sidewalk proud and sassy, they'd stop barking dreckly and admire him no end. Some of 'em would give a hind leg to live a while his fashion and know all he does about the hills."

Marlen wasn't dumb. He studied me, thoughtfully. "You think, honest, it would be thataway?"

"I'm dead positive," I said. "Why man, they'd hang around in Sam's store all night listening to—uh—Rusty's stories about the caves he's found, and the old Indian stuff you were telling me about, and all those other yarns about the woods and rocks. I know it would be that way. Suppose you give it a try, Marlen, a good honest try—and tell me about it when I get back to the hills next time."

Smoky and the Golden Vixen

MY goodness, how that young vixen fox hated my black dog Smoky! She despised the ground he walked on. She wished he'd fall down dead. Or go 'way off across the hills and break all four of his legs. Every time he showed up over there around her whelping den and biddies, you should have heard the riot act she read him.

But Smoke was an amiable fellow and didn't mind. A European-type pinscher, somewhat smaller but more sturdily built than the American breed, he was an exceedingly friendly, gentle dog, though a deadly fighter when he had to fight. He had his own reasons—which he tried to tell me about but couldn't—for hanging around that den, and he didn't care one hoot about the bad names the vixen called him.

Her habit of ticking Smoke off was what first put me onto the odd situation over on that briar hillside, across a little valley from my house. Into my study window one May afternoon drifted the unmistakable sounds of a vixen fox trying to scare some intruder away from her den and cubs. She kept it up so long that I concluded she must be

in serious trouble and might need help, so I got my glasses
and rifle, whistled for Smoke—but he'd gone off somewhere—and headed over in that direction, taking care to
keep out of sight and approach from down wind.

I had a hunch that the den I'd find her at was a certain
one which I'd passed many times and knew well. In the
middle of a two-acre open spot, it had originally been a
woodchuck burrow, like most fox dens. One of the entrances had been enlarged fox-size, and no doubt a big
lay-up chamber had been excavated back inside. The old
signs all around showed that vixens for many fox generations had favored the place as their whelping den. To a
gravid female fox who felt her time approaching and was
looking for a home, the place had its strong points. A fine
mousing swamp just down the hill meant a handy food
supply for her family; the apron of dirt at the entrance
provided cubs with a dust bath, so needed to keep down
mites and fleas; and the hillside was well isolated from
farm houses and farm dogs.

A hundred yards away I eased up behind a rock, rose
up carefully and drew the den close with my binoculars.
At the entrance I saw three fuzzy little heads sticking out,
their ears cocked, their attitude one of bug-eyed curiosity.
At the first warning bark of a vixen watching over her
young, a litter of cubs go swishing into the den, *zip, zip,
zip,* but those three little imps had got over their fright
and now were trying to see what their mommy was scold-
ing so about.

At the edge of a small woods a few rods to the right I spotted the vixen, up in a squat, leaning sassafras tree, and recognized her at once. A trim, smallish red fox, with so much yellow in her fur that in bright sunlight she seemed washed with gold, she was still another instance of that very pretty color phase which I have mentioned previously. Often I had glimpsed this vixen along that briar ridge and had watched her mousing in the valley swamp the previous winter, and I knew her well.

Though they are creatures of the night, foxes often go hunting on murky winter afternoons, in times of hunger; and if you get a chance to watch one mousing, let your other business wait. You'll see a piece of outdoor artistry. The cat, hawk or owl never lived that could match a fox's expertness at mousing afield.

About forty feet above the den I saw something black lying in the sedge grass, and put the glasses on it. Blow me down, it was Smoke! Now and then he would look over toward the angry vixen as if to say, "Woman, for goodness sake relax. I don't aim on harming your precious bairns." When one of the cubs would venture out onto the dirt apron, he would watch it and wag his tail amiably as though saying: "Howd'y, little fellow. Don't be afraid. It's just me."

The dog-fox was nowhere around. I knew him also, a big red, with a run as swift and airy as a plover's skimming. When he didn't show up at all, in what happened later, I realized he was dead. Sometime after the mating period in January he'd got killed and the vixen was rearing the cubs by herself. And that was quite a job. She not only had to bring in food for the ravenous little things but had to stand vigilant guard over them every hour of the day and night.

Smoke's friendliness and feeling of kinship toward the vixen and cubs, indeed toward all foxes, would ordinarily have been unnatural in a dog, but in his particular case it was entirely understandable. When he was a small pup I brought in a wild fox cub only a few weeks old, to make a household pet of it, and the two of them grew up together as playmates and companions. They tumbled around on the lawn together, had the same ideas about my bedroom slippers, slept together in a nail-keg nest, and when their legs got long enough they'd go tootling off together on juvenile hunting expeditions.

Being much the larger of the two, Smoke developed a protective attitude toward Flash and often he stood off dogs which had the idea that foxes is foxes. For well over a year they were almost inseparable, and when a farmer down valley shot Flash one day, Smoke was downcast and at loose ends for a long while afterward.

Later, when Smoke was five years old, I brought in another tiny fox cub and Smoke adopted it on sight. He always carefully licked it from head to tail when we got through feeding it, and when I'd pretend to be angry at the little thing, Smoke got so distressed that he'd crawl under the bed and whimper, the big goof. When Swifty grew up enough, Smoke proudly led it out mousing and hunting, very much as a dog-wolf will teach its young. When Swifty was about a year old he began going back to the wild, mostly because some dogs up the road persecuted him so much; but for another year he would come around to the back door for a handout at lean times, and I knew that he and Smoke frequently met outdoors and had a run together, till finally Swifty too met some disaster and vanished.

So that was why Smoke, amiable and good-natured to begin with, was friendly toward foxes. To him a fox was just a small, queerish dog that didn't come in to dinner. When he flushed a wild fox in the fields or woods he would stand and watch it disappear, and you could see he was puzzled no end by its fleeing from him. I'm sure he never did figure out why the vixen called him those bad names when he went over there. I suppose he felt she was just one of those fuss-budgets and let it go at that.

Well, if Smoke was dumb about the vixen, I was equally dumb about Smoke. At that time I was buried in work and couldn't go out country-side with him very much, and I just imagined he was a bit lonely and went over there to be around "folks." Undoubtedly his desire for association did figure in his hanging around over yonder, but his main reason for visiting that fox family was something different, something I didn't catch onto till it hit me bang over the head.

Watching Flash and Smoke grow up together under

identical conditions confirmed an opinion I had already formed from observing foxes in the wild: that they are not naturally as smart as dogs, as I have mentioned before. Of course a fox that is well trained and educated, which means that his full potential is developed, makes the average dog seem like a lunkhead. And of course a fox is quicker, flashier and more agile than a dog, and in some forms of hunting he is incomparably sharper and more efficient. But the over-all picture is that foxes are less pliable, less versatile, harder to teach tricks, harder to housebreak, slower to catch onto things.

But a fox is smart enough, and under the right circumstances it does make a unique pet and an enjoyable four-footed companion. Pretty and graceful creatures, they are wonderfully adroit at catching balls, doing ladder stunts and all the jumping tricks. But they are very freedom-loving animals and must be allowed to come and go. Even more than other creatures, a fox on a chain or in a cage is not a companion but a prisoner, and it develops a bad disposition, even as you or I would. The fox you see at a zoo or tied up at a filling station is a pitiful caricature of the dainty, affectionate creature that likes to go to sleep on your lap or cuts figure-eights of joy when you go out of the house to take it on a country hike.

When I walked on up to the den, I whistled Smoke to me and told him that he should stay away from that place and quit disturbing that fox family. He understood me all right, but he always had a mind of his own, Smoke did, and when he felt strongly that I was wrong about something, he did things *his* way. So he simply stood there wagging his tail in that short, jerky fashion which meant, "I'm not a-going to do it, guy," so I left him there and he didn't come home till nearly dusk.

The next afternoon he came into my study, nudged my arm and importuned me to go out country-gadding with him. This was pretty much routine with us, each afternoon. If I told him, "In a little while, fellow," he would wait patiently till I knocked off. Sometimes I would say, "Can't go today, Smoke; gotta work." I'm sure it puzzled him how anybody with good sense could sit at a desk and make bug tracks on paper when the sunny fields and cool green hills were beckoning. But he never argued. When I told him I had to work, he would turn and leave and go take a country rounds by himself.

This time, though, he came in an hour earlier than usual and also he would hardly take no for an answer. Three or four times he came back into the study and argued with me to go along with him. Later on I remembered this unusual insistence of his and wondered— Did he, in his inarticulate way, want me and my rifle along with him over there at that fox den? I can't say positively but I do believe that's what was in his mind.

However that may be, he trotted across to the den by himself and was there for two, three hours. And every day after that when I couldn't go hiking with him, he went over there and spent a good part of the afternoon,

asleep as often as not. The vixen always gave him a chewing out when he first showed up, but after some days she
would fuss at him for only a few minutes, then would lie
silent in the sassafras and keep an eye on him and her
bairns.

The cubs got so they would come out and play while
he was there, but they wouldn't come near him or let
him get close to them. His memories of Flash and Swifty
were pleasant and strong, I know, and he must have been
disappointed by the fox family's refusal to associate with
him.

I kept wondering why the vixen didn't move somewhere else. Almost invariably they will abandon a den
that is molested or even visited one time by an enemy, and
down valley there was a nice, inviting woodland, with
buckbrush slopes and plenty of groundhog holes. But the
vixen stayed on in spite of Smoke's repeated visits.

In a couple of weeks she began taking her cubs out
hunting with her, in the early whippoorwill dusk, and
what eager, proud-stepping little tikes they were as they
trotted along behind, beside and sometimes under her.
Down at the swamp she taught them to catch frogs and
mice, but always she brought them back to the whelping
den for the day.

When Smoke finally stopped going over there I knew
that the fox family had abandoned the den, according to
fox custom, and were lying out the days in some scatter
of woods or deerbush, with a hole handy for the cubs to

pop into. By this time I was aware that something out of the ordinary had been going on over there and I'd made some guesses about it, all wide of the mark. "But now," I thought, "it's over with, whatever was bothering him."

That was another bad guess. It wasn't over with by a mile and a toad hop, that little drama on that briar hillside.

During the summer I glimpsed the swiftly growing cubs a few times, mostly around brooks and small ponds where frogs are plentiful. Frogs are easy to catch, and young foxes, not yet expert hunters, go for them in a big way, along with lots of insects and berries. But in late August the cubs seemed to disappear, one by one. When I didn't hear them calling at night, during September and October, I knew definitely that they hadn't survived those first perilous months on their own. I felt sorry to see them vanish. In that part of the valley foxes had been all but wiped out, and now they were down to just one—the vixen. In spite of her dumbness about Smoke, she was a very smart fox, as smart as I've ever trailed and observed. That's why she survived where the others died.

About this night calling of young foxes—they do a lot of it in the fall. I don't know what the reason is, unless it's just that they're bursting with vitality. This night call, given on the dead run, is a downright eerie sound; eerie and wild and what-on-earth-is-*that?* Drawn out and somewhat like the cry of a red-throated loon, you hear it go floating across a dark field or along a ridgeline at the speed of a skimming bird—so fast that most people won't believe

247

you that it's a fox. It certainly comes near being that "disembodied voice" the poet speaks of.

When the first snows came and I was censusing the rabbits over in that direction, I often came across the trail of my pretty, trim vixen, and the mousing swamp was a network of her dainty, straight-in-line tracks. Foxes are great mousers, and meadow mice (*Microtus*) are their main diet item. As many a field study has showed, they prey very little on game. My own data indicates that ten mice per night is minimum for a fox. That means they destroy several thousand mice a year, and considering the extensive damage that mice can do to a pasture, the person who kills off the foxes on his place without special reason isn't playing it very smart.

In early January the vixen was joined by a dog-fox for about two weeks. Again and again Smoke and I came upon their trails leading along together, through mile after mile of the winter-stilled woods and barren fields. In all likelihood this dog-fox came from some hills several miles away, but what happened to him after the mating fortnight I don't know. He may have gone back to his native hills. More likely he walked into that damnable oblivion which had taken all the valley foxes except my golden vixen.

At any rate he vanished, and the vixen ranged alone again and faced the challenge again of raising a brood of young by herself.

Coming home one twilight in March, Smoke and I happened to pass within a few hundred feet of the old whelping den, and the vixen began circling us out in the dark and trying to frighten us away. They seldom do this in the daytime but at twilight or after night they invariably do it. They'll come out and meet you as much as a thousand feet from the burrow and let loose a spate of throaty little barks, howls, moans, and a sequence that sounds exactly like a man gagging. It's a scary business if you don't know what it is, but it turns a bit pathetic when you know they're merely trying, in the only way they have, to keep you away from their home and bairns.

I suspected the vixen was using that den again, and Smoke and I swung over past there to see what. I didn't have to look at the telltale tracks and other signs. Smoke took a whiff at the entrance and then stood there with his ears cocked, listening, wagging his tail, and I knew he was hearing the mewing of newborn cubs back in that lay-up chamber.

"Here," I thought, "is where we go again."

And go again we did. Every day that I couldn't go out with him, Smoke trotted over there and put in a couple or three hours lying in the sedge. When he asked to be let out the kitchen door my housekeeper used to chide him about the "affair" he was carrying on over yonder, and several other people had the same idea. This was altogether wrong. There wasn't one iota of sex interest in Smoke's visits over there.

In about a month the cubs, five of them this time, began coming out on warm sunny days. I wanted one of them the worst old way, and knew Smoke would be pleased as pups with it; but I was planning to be in the North for a couple of months later on, and my housekeeper took a dim view of looking after a "wild animal." However, the den was a favorable one to watch, and I got in several sessions with a mounted glass from a small rise just across the swamp. A study of fox family life under absolutely natural conditions like that is a rare occurrence, and also a litter of fox cubs, the highest-strung little scamps outdoors, put on a show worth kibitzing. If they weren't pouncing on crickets or grasshoppers or tumbling around in play, they were stalking imaginary prey, nibbling at green stuff or staging one of their innumerable little spit-fights.

Then, one evening, Smoke came home limping in a foreleg and chewed up a bit otherwise. It was plain he'd been in a dog fight, and I concluded that he'd had a run-in with a pair of vicious dogs which belonged to the farmer down valley and which roamed the countryside doing such things as nosing out rabbit nests, killing small game, occasionally killing a fawn. When I went over to the den the next morning everything seemed as usual, the five cubs playing in the sun, the vixen eying me from the ridgeline. There were no signs of a fight but I knew in my bones that those two dogs had tried to swoop in on the cubs and Smoke had tied into them.

I had already figured that the cubs of the previous year

had fallen victim to the guns and traps of the gentleman down valley, and now I began to understand a couple of the other puzzles. The vixen had been afraid of those dogs, instinctively afraid of the whole range down there, and that was why she didn't move her cubs to that better cover. And Smoke, knowing that the dogs often roamed up along that ridge, had been aware that they constituted a danger to those small Flashes and Swiftys over there and so had assumed a sort of guardianship over the den, very much as he had guarded his two fox companions. The protective instinct runs strong in any well-raised and emotionally mature dog, and you can double that for the pinscher blood.

Right here I want to state my personal opinion that the pinscher's reputation for savageness is a libel on a fine breed. To be sure, they can be trained to be savage, but so can any dog. And true, they are wicked fighters, especially the sturdy European type. Smoke could kill an ordinary dog his size with a lunge and a throat slash. Only, he never fought. When I took him along into town I often felt ashamed of the way any waspish little pennyfeist could back him off the sidewalk. But that's the way I'd trained him and that's the way I wanted him.

After that first skirmish, things turned peaceful again for a little while. In fact, Smoke and I had several good belly-laughs over on that hillside. I was doing some groundhog dispersion study that spring, along with analyzing stomach contents for an economic appraisal of the woodchuck, and sometimes I would take a groundhog carcass to the fox den, lay it near the entrance and then get back to watch, with Smoke.

The cubs, weaned by now, would smell the fresh meat and come piling out of the den, and straightaway they would stage one of those dizzy, noisy, roundhouse fights. The sassiest little imps outdoors, fox cubs fight incessantly even when there's nothing to fight about, and when you put down some fresh meat and they come boiling out, there's blood on the moon right now. With diminutive snarls, yips, yowls, hisses, barks and *kaa-acks*, they sail into one another headlong, everybody biting everybody, and about all you can see is a peck or so of legs, heads and fuzzy bodies, in a state of violent agitation. I've seen these half-pint battles last ten minutes and wind up a hundred feet down hill.

When Smoke wasn't over there the vixen stayed close to the den and kept a watchful eye over her bairns. This watch-and-ward of a mother fox is one of the prettiest sights in nature. There's something elemental and timeless about it that gets at you. The cubs tumble around, chase butterflies, get into trouble, watch a passing buzzard with the curiosity of innocent childhood, while the mother fox lies on a sentinel rock, or calls a warning if the buzzard turns out to be an eagle, or goes walking proudly around through her irresponsible little flock. Proudly? You can see pride in her manner, her every move.

Then, one evening, Smoke failed to come in at dinnertime. As the night wore on and no Smoke, I began to worry about him, and I was much relieved, near midnight, to hear his familiar scratch and "Woof" at the back door. I think he must have come home earlier but hung around out in the yard, afraid I'd give him a talking to for fighting, as I usually did.

For he had been in a nasty battle and was a sorry sight —his ears slashed, his hide full of briars and crab thorns, his fur blood-soaked, his legs bitten and badly swollen. I fixed him up the best I could, gave him a sedative and took him to the veterinary early the next morning.

Back home, I hurried across to the fox den to see what had happened. Before I got there I saw the buzzards circling. A hundred feet below the den two of the cubs lay dead in the grass and pennyroyal. The vixen had carried a third cub, probably with a little life still in it, back to the den, but it had died and she had laid it on the apron of dirt.

Just out the hillside from the two dead cubs, one of the roaming dogs, its throat torn out, had staggered into some briars and toppled over.

The story, as I reconstructed it, was that the two dogs had caught the cubs off base, down the hill, and made a swoop at them. For some reason, possibly because he was just then leaving to come home, Smoke hadn't been able to intercept the dogs; otherwise he would certainly have stood them off till the cubs got back to the den. But he did get into the picture in time to save two of them. The one dog, a black and tan mongrel slightly smaller than himself, he had killed on the spot. The other dog, a big, formidable Chow . . . Later that day I drove around to the farm down valley, on some pretext, and learned that the Chow had managed to crawl back home, but he was slashed and torn and the farmer had shot him.

It would be pleasant to report that after Smoke's valiant defense of her cubs the vixen realized he was a friend and became more companionable towards him. Alas, that wasn't the case. In her eyes Smoke had been there at the time of the killing and understandably she didn't distinguish between him and the other dogs. When he got out and around again and ambled over there, she gave him the usual chewing out.

The gentleman down valley moved away that summer and the farmer who bought him out destroyed the box-traps and suchlike and took a civilized attitude toward the wildlife on his place. So the two young foxes that Smoke had saved survived the summer. When fall came, Smoke and I would sit out on the front porch at night and hear their eerie barking over on the ridge, and I know that Smoke was wishing they'd come on over and associate with him, as Flash and Swifty used to do.